A COLLECTION OF POEMS, STORIES AND
OBSERATIONS BY

K. L.

Bravin Publishing, LLC

Published by
Bravin Publishing, LLC
Brooklyn, New York

All poems are original works by the author.

ISBN -13: 978-0-615-20514-4
ISBN -10: 0-615-20514-3

Cover and Interior Designed by
The Writer's Assistant
www.thewritersassisant.com

Printed in the United States of America

CONTENTS

ACKNOWLEDGMENTS

Lord, I want to thank You, first, for saving my life and allowing me to turn the corner. I am traveling the road You laid out for me and I am no longer afraid.

Tiffany, my lovely supportive friend and my wife, I would not be the man I am without you in my life. Thank you, babe, and I love you with every fiber of my heart!

To my children, please allow this book to show you that there are always higher heights to reach if you trust in God.

I want to, especially, thank my mother, grandmother, and sisters. What would I be without all of you? We never had much, however love saw us through. This book is as much for you as it is for me. Thank you. I love you!

To my partners, T.J., John, and Curt, who would always ask, "Is the book finished?" Well, here it is fellas! We're in the game now!

To all of my students, please understand there is nothing on this planet that can stop you if you have faith in yourselves and the Lord up above. Take the talent God gave you and run with it, never to look back or doubt yourselves. I love each and every one of you.

A sincere thank you to my spiritual sister sent from the Lord to help me along this path, Daphine Glenn Robinson, author of *Brotherly Love & Betrayal.* From the moment you reached out to me on Myspace.com, I knew you were heaven sent. Your advice and motivation was never lost.

Thank you Tiah Short and Martin Pratt of Urban Literary Review for putting out the best information about the writing game on your show each week, on Blogtalkradio.com, and your websites. I have learned so much and appreciate the help and support. Thank you, Ella Curry, for showing me how a professional writer has to be. Each week your show, Black-Authors-Network on Blogtalkradio.com, is a vessel disseminating fantastic information to world. Thank you all for giving me the opportunity to showcase my talents.

Finally, I would like to thank everyone who chose my book to read. You have made my dreams come true. If we ever meet, you will understand the reason for the BIG HUGS AND BIG SMILE! Please enjoy every word.

INTRODUCTION

As a man travels through life, many things affect the way he chooses to walk his path. Some may run and see nothing, some may quit and stay right where they are, and others will grow as they walk, taking in each moment as they pass by. *A Man in Transition* is a reflection of my path and the variables that have affected my steps. I was never a child who considered God would bless me with the talent to write anything on this scale. However, as you grow and mature, you start to have many experiences in your life. The Lord's voice grows stronger and, even if you travel in a different direction, you will still experience what He wants for you. However, it will not make as much sense until you give in and listen. There is love and emotion that comes along the way as your life takes shapes—the love you have for God, your children, and, of course, finding a good woman. There is passion for the same things. There is reflection when you take the time to look back and ask yourself the hard questions. *A Man in Transition* will give you all that, and so much more.

K. L.

A glimpse into my world, *A Man in Transition* is written from my heart. I wanted to share my love, pain, joys and sorrows with you. Like most men, I have lived through certain parts of my body instead of stepping up and becoming the husband, son, brother, and father God designed me to be. The trials and tribulations we all talk about are real. However, there are other sights on this traveled road. The spiritual man, romantic, parent, urban teacher and how I see the world through my travels are expressed within these pages. One particular piece I struggled with putting in the book, which had to do with my past way of living. I wasn't quite sure how it would be accepted or perceived. However, one thing I did know for sure was that many church folks would have issues with my choice of words. But, I asked myself if I could really show my true transition without showing my past. Therefore, the last chapter reflects my old way of thinking. In that final section, you will walk with me as my words express my thirst for the physical part that many men live and ultimately die for.

Many people write for various reasons. My motivation was my children and the students I have taught. It was important that I instill in my children that as long as they had true faith in God, anything was possible. To my students, I needed to teach them how no matter what their weaknesses were they could accomplish anything. English was my worst subject in school. I learned to get around the fact I did not like to read. My seventh grade English teacher, Mr. Goldberg, said, "Keith, you are the worst thing your mother ever had!" Now here I am, a teacher and I wrote this book, the start of my endless literary journey. Please enjoy and, as with anything else, give this a second read and see if you can feel my emotions in each poem, story or rant.

I am a child of God. I have turned my life over to the Lord and with each project I undertake, I would like my readers to know the role the Lord played, and continues to play, in my life. Money is not my motivation, rather the idea of having people reading my words. So, if you're reading this, thank you for making my dreams come true.

Sit back and take your time. I truly believe you will find something inside these pages that will touch your soul. *A Man in Transition* is a labor of love and an example of what can happen when you trust those around you who say, you can do it. Through poetry, storytelling and ranting, I want you to take your place inside my heart and mind. As you read, please observe the highs and lows of this man. This was not easy to write simply because it is not about a distant person, place or thing. It is about me—"K. L.," Keith B. to most, and Mr. B to my many students. It is my first step in allowing the world to see what makes me who I am.

If you are looking for something to touch you, then this is the book for you. I have no formal training as a writer. I simply sit down at the computer and allow God to take my hands. For it was through the Lord's grace that saved my life and allowed me to present this book to you.

K. L.

My steps with God and my steps without him are here. My love, my passions and my failures are written within these pages.

CHAPTER 1

Spiritually

These are the Words of a Man Saved by the Lord.

Each selection shows my connection to our Father in Heaven. We all have to make choices in our lives and for me, choosing Jesus Christ saved my life. These words were birthed from that experience.

These poems are my opportunity to show you what the Lord is doing in my life. Yes, I am a born again Christian. I am a believer that Jesus Christ died for my sins, which allows my salvation. I try to absorb the words of the Bible and use them as an anchor to becoming and remaining a new person. I'm living a life that has more meaning these days. Trying to be an example of what a man should be to everyone, I meet. I want everyone to know and understand one thing. Men do change. With these words, I am saying loudly, yes some of us are cheaters, liars, haters, thieves and have done such negatives that many thought there was no hope. However, given the right circumstances, the right love, and forgiveness, and with God's grace, we will humble ourselves and change. I pray faith echoes in my words. Enjoy the spirit as I see and feel it.

A PASSIONATE MAN

My very first poem written in 2000

It is a passionate man who works the extra hours.

A man for no reason brings his mother flowers.

It is a passionate man who looks upon his children as
    priceless.

A man who understands when others have been
    thoughtless.

It is a passionate man who loves you without fear.

A man who craves you and keeps you near.

It is a passionate man that, even at the end, will still have
    your hand.

Please, God. Please help me to one day be a Passionate
    Man.

DON'T PASS ME BY

Through the eyes of the homeless

You gaze at me as if my face has no features; there is a
human underneath all this.

So you're better than me, as if this was my dream when I
skipped to school along side you.

Look deeper, we are not that different, we are only a few
mistakes away from each other.

*

Food has lost its taste. I eat to survive. Can you relate as
you order lunch?

How dare you think I don't have feelings, try laying here
on a cold winter's night?

Get a job you say, how come it's never, "Do you need some
help?" You're quick to tell but not to offer.

*

Abuse comes in many forms, some I allowed and others I
didn't sign up for.

Ever fought for a bed, food, sneakers or your pride, and
then told you're worthless?

Your God may be good to you, but look up at a large dark
sky, in the middle of a cold night, starving, and you'll
question, does He truly exist?

*

3

Well, I have to go, the shelter gives a whole sandwich
   today, plus I can see your Latté is getting cold.
Keep me in mind when you say to your children, "Don't
   waste, people are starving in Africa." Guess what, we're
   really not that far away.
Please pray along with me as I ask that someday you'll stop
   and talk to me, since you don't hear me when I scream,
   Don't pass me by!!

*How fast do we pass the homeless only to act as if we
don't see or hear their cries for help? We act as though
they are not our brothers and sisters who have fallen on
hard times.*

Remember what the Bible says:
Hebrews 13:
1. Keep on loving each other as brothers.
*2. Do not forget to entertain strangers, for by so doing
some people have entertained angels without knowing it.*

RAIN IN THE CITY

Here we are again, Father.

Another night in the city You created and lead me to rest
    my head in.
The place where the noise can be deafening, but the subtle
    breeze reminds me You're there.
The rain washes away the anger and filth, leaving the gift of
    design given to the men You've saved.

At night is when I feel closer to You, no crowds no sounds.
It is at this time, I allow my mind to dance with the
    thoughts of what You have blessed me with.
Each raindrop is a quick reminder that You can see all and
    underneath all is Your presence.

Each step is filled with visions of my past and a future not
    seen
As I rest on this bench, I am taken in that You are my
    guide and You're in control
It is not sadness I feel but an uneasy happiness as if this is
    wrong, but I know it's not.

K. L.

As I rise up to make my way home, I pay tribute to all You
   have done.
The rain is cleansing my soul, which a person needs in a
   city this big.
As I stroll along these wet streets, my smile is bright for I
   am blessed.

I love the fact that each day You grant the chance to say,
   Here we are again, Father.

I HAVE SEEN THE DEVIL AND HE IS ME

This man I am I don't know who he is, yet I have his
  memories.
His sprit can't be the one I own.
How do you explain my actions in this world God created?
Wasn't I supposed to be more than what I am? There must
  be something wrong.
The pain I have inflicted on others can't be what the Lord
  designed for me.
The lies I have told came too natural from my lips.
Women are not toys put here for my amusement.
Children are to be cared for not created and left.
Lord, as great as you are can You free me?
I am weary of this waste of life I am.
I was told God will forgive me if I am truly ready to
  allow Him.
On my knees I cry and pray,
Please, God, save me!
I have seen the devil and he is me.

***There comes that time when you have to face what you
are and humbly admit your guilt to be truly free. This is
one of the first steps to regaining your soul.***

LIES

Advice for my brothers and sisters

My advice brothers,
Every time you lie, you give the devil something to
    work with.
He takes that lie and applies pressure to your mind, body
    and soul.
You find yourself drifting farther away from your true self.
Slowly becoming more of what you are not.
Lies are the tools of evil.
Why become the handyman of the most feared and
    despised.
In every man, there is the fight to not give in to the
    transition lies cause.
A man's strength is forged in his connection to self, family
    and a good woman.
Even with all that, many men embrace the evil that makes
    them less than human.
So, with every untruth uttered from our lips we do the
    devil's works even when our souls scream stop!
My advice sisters,
Look closely at that man, listen to his words, and compare
    his actions to the things he says. If you look deep, you

can see the Devil at work. Pray you see it in time.
The Lies of man can corrupt every part of your soul if you
allow them to plant seed in your heart.

*We have to control our mouths the best we can. What we
say can be the undoing of who we are.*

*James 1:26: If anyone considers himself religious and
yet does not keep a tight rein on his tongue, he deceives
himself and his religion is worthless.*

MISTAKES

Don't we hurt and learn from them?
Can we become better people because of them?
Is there a way to avoid and control them?
My life has its share of them.
The path I travel upon has the remembrance of many of
    them!
I have spent many sleepless nights wondering why do I
    keep repeating
The pain I try to hide from is a result of them.
I have walked through many wrong doors by not paying
    attention to other's stories about them.
It's now clear that I'm not alone, many suffer from them.
So time to stop hating and understand it is a part of life to
    make them.
The strength of a true man comes from his ability to rise
    above them.
The love and support I have from so many is my shield
    against them.
I have begun to understand that some of the greatest
    accomplishments were the outcome of them.
The man I have become has prepared me for them.
Then God touched me, he said,

"My son, I made you and I don't make them,"
Mistakes.

K. L.

WELCOME HOME

Dedicated to Ms. De Bella, an Art teacher,
who lost her battle to cancer.

Don't be afraid, it was your time.
The time for pain has passed.
Your days of worry are no longer.
I have seen the greatness of your work.

Welcome Home

Your efforts were not in vain; you'll not be forgotten.
The seeds of your wisdom are safely tucked away in your
    students.
Your soul can rest with the knowledge your best was done.
Be at peace.

Welcome Home

Yes heads will lower today, don't worry.
Your artwork will remind them each day of your passion.
The lives you've reached are brighter.
Come rest your head.

Welcome Home

12

As you see, the stories were true.
So frolic with peace and joy.
Feel no sadness, for others are here to join you in your stay.
This is a place for love and rejoicing.

Welcome Home

To the others left behind, your love will serve as a guide.
When you want, place a loving glance down on the rest of
    your family and friends.
Your talents are needed here.
So from today until forever, rest you have earned it.

K. L.

Gone, But Not Forgotten

My arms are open as if they remember on their own.
When I rest, I still expect to awake to that smile in the
kitchen.
I sometimes think that's you calling when I hear the phone
ring.

I see you, when I look in my mirror.
There are days that I am lost and have no answers now that
you're gone.
My life is wrapped with the magic that was your love.

These tears are to affirm the love that will exist in my soul
forever.
What I wouldn't give for one more kiss upon my forehead.
I had doubts I could make it but yet I am firm.

I am now the mother and my children are me.
Your words spring from my mouth, for today I understand.
My vision is shaped by the time spent watching, learning
and sharing.

God needed you so I never questioned.
I am strong and proud to have had you with me.

To my mother, I yell with remorse, faith and love, you are

Gone, but not forgotten

Dedicated to my mother-in-law written from what I saw in my ex-wife's eyes. I know she loved her mother with all her heart. Just because you're not with a person anymore doesn't mean you hurt less when they hurt. My ex-wife is still the mother of my children and her pain affects everyone who knows her. This is my offer of comfort and testimony.

TIME TO REST

It's time to unclench your fist and let the pain go; you have
lost someone special.
Their journey home is complete.
You should let go and keep that person in your prayers.
A greater force needs their time and their name has been
called.
Your eyes and heart will speak for you today as they fill
with sorrow.
In the end, a smile and joy will be the outcome of the
memories left behind.

The clouds will look a little different from now on, a hint
of the smile they had.
So look up and see right there, sits someone you love.
I know you feel alone with your pain and the thought of
losing someone special surrounds you.
Understand, you haven't loss anything; you have gained
another to welcome you home when it's your time.

Let your voice not quiver, nor shake, this was pre-arranged.
Rejoice at the time you shared and memories that remain.
Each night speak to the Lord, say to him, Thank you father
for filling me with so much joy.

The hurt was great but I'll be okay because knowing they're with you.

In the morning, spring to your feet understanding that it's time to make the Lord proud of you all over again.

Reach out to the others who don't know how our Holy Father works, for they may be confused.

They won't understand how you can be happy instead of sad during these difficult days.

With the biggest smile and hardest hug, let them know your still here for them and they need not worry the Lord had this planned.

It's time to unclench your fist and let the pain go. You have lost someone special. With a loud sigh, rest easy knowing they have been called by GOD, who will greet them saying, "Time to Rest my child!"

MY FATHER I AM READY

Beloved Father, forgive my fall,
I didn't know I was meant to inherit it all.
In this world, You are my light.
Without your word, the evil would corrupt my sight.

King of Kings, reach down and touch me
Cause the Naysayer to flee.
I stand on your promise, for your promises are true,
I kneel and humbly ask what should I do?

Your son shed his blood so that I might live,
In return, it's my soul I shall give.
Others have come after him but fell as man
Do we really understand that was part of your plan?

Prophet after Prophet came to share the news,
So why do we act as if we have no clue?
Salvation for all is tied to Your grace,
This is the reason we, Your children, strive to see Your
     face.

Father, I know death is only a starting point of my
     journey home,

But, my fear is that I may end up alone.
Father, You said by Faith is the only way to reach You,
But, when you know you're a sinner what can you do?

Like David, Elijah, Peter and Paul,
change me and bless me, to keep me from ending up
    like Sampson, Judas or Saul.
My Faith is growing and my learning is steady,
all because on judgment day I want to be able to say,
MY FATHER I AM READY

To Be a Different Me

It took re-opened eyes to accept what I hadn't become,
    instead to see what I really was.
Future dreams fell on thoughts of what is, what could be
    and settling.
Walking in the footsteps of greatness means that
    mediocrity can't be the norm.
If I am to be a different me.

Pleasure and accomplishment require focus and cannot be
    replaced with fear of failure.
Motivation should have her time to dance and not be
    seated in bondage like that of doubt.
Joy and song has to spring forth like the Sun each
    morning, unlike Gloom and forced silence that follows
    the Dark Storms.
If I am to be a different me.

Friends have to be welcomed and savored like the taste of
    a great meal, not cast out or removed like bitter herbs
    and soured wine.
Comfort has to be found in the One most powerful and
    you cannot convince yourself that you are all you need.

Love has to be met with great aspiration and worth, not to
be pushed away and shut out as if her warmth will
burn.
If I am to be a different me.

Age is to be met with grace as that of old paintings, not
with sorrowful thoughts of what could have been.
The future is open to all and has many benefits, only if it's
looked upon as gracious and not damning.
You can become everything the you allow yourself to be,
but you will become exactly what you create for yourself
as you wonder,
If I am to be a different me.

YOU WON'T HAVE ME SATAN FOR MY FATHER IS NEAR!

My knees, legs are sore and tears fill my eyes, you have touched this body but not my soul. With each passing day, I know the lord hears my cries and prayers. I am touched by the spirit and to it, I hold tight. The ideas of your madness will not invade me, your wonders are vast but greater is my Lord

Take this body, and all that I have. For my Father has more than I could ever want or need and so to you I laugh. The pain you cause only forces me to grow stronger in faith, for what I lack in health I gain in blessing. Continue your assault on all that is righteous, you and I both know what the outcome will be in the end of time.

The word is my guide and my belief is strong, so your anger will only serve to move me along. You were there once and you know the place I am bound for, so try and keep me from it. The father won't allow it and he sends word of what is to be.

So up I stare for the face of strength and humility and righteousness is there. While below, you plot and plan to destroy all that is his. You don't grow tired of the defeats at his hands. So do what you were sent here to do. Take what you will take from me.

The word tells me I am not alone, that you're a liar. So you're gifts I don't want, Your cures I won't indulge, your women I don't need and the pain is only temporary for a better place is prepared for me. You can only cause my existence here to be difficult but never impossible for the true Power rest with my Father and it is he that whispers in my ear, ***"MY SON, WHEN YOU SEE THE MOST DESPISED, TELL HIM THIS FROM YOUR GRACIOUS FATHER FROM ON HIGH."***

You won't have me Satan for my Father is near!

CHAPTER 2

Romance

When a man opens up and allows his heart to speak,
this is what you'll find.

There is a romantic side of man. The part of him he may only allow a few to see and share. Many aren't aware of what truly lies at the depths of the heart of each and every man. These poems and stories should make it so much clearer.

Romance, oh man where do I start? I've always been a romantic guy at heart. Even when I was at the worst that I could be, I considered myself a romantic. I think every player believes that he is a romantic even though he might be a hound at heart. It's sad, but many men believe there is something romantic about trying to be that lady's man. Real romance comes when you truly find someone you respect enough to want to search love with them. There is nothing like it. In many of these poems, that feeling was inspired by my lovely new wife. You'll also get a sense of the romance that men create when out and about thinking the hunt causes the romance to come out. At the heart of it all, I truly

24

believed I was the essence of a romantic. This may sound funny coming from a man, I really did and still do believe in concept of love. I think love is the second greatest gift that God has ever given to us. The first is life itself. Think about it, romance is the wedding veil to love. When you get to the moment of lifting it, look what you're left with. Okay, I am still basking in the memories of my wedding. Another way to look at it is romance is the appetizer to love. When you really have love as your objective, the romance becomes so much better. You just find yourself doing things that might not seem right to anybody else, but it definitely seems right to you, if true love is at the basis of what you are trying to become. I find that when you allow yourself to sink into it romance becomes something incredible. As you read these poems and stories, my wish is that you can see that. You might have to read this section a couple of times, or at least I ask you to, okay?

PERFECT WOMAN
If Only in My Mind

I ask myself, why I am so lucky? Is there a reason I am so
blessed?

But, you're never supposed to question God's work. I say
God because how do you explain her patience with me.

There is something about the way she understands my
needs.

Are there other women who would love another's children
like her own?

Would another woman be strong enough to trust God and
take you back when you have tasted someone else's
fruits?

Her soul is pure enough to douse the evil that once filled
my own.

My vanity, pride and smugness have been replaced with
concern, endearment and gratefulness.

I now concern myself with more than just my own needs.

Her smile fills my heart with joy.

Her tears burn at my soul and demand my immediate
attention or screams for forgiveness.

I am blessed with an equal, so again I ask why I am so
lucky.

Does God see something in me I don't see? He must.

She is sexy beyond belief, even when she sleeps.

Can that comfortable look come from what I have brought
to her life?

The world is funny, one minute you're all alone, next thing
all your dreams are being answered.

Thank you, God!

Well the only course of action is to leave all my worries,
fears, and concerns at God's feet.

Something about having the right woman makes each day,
night and morning special.

I really do have the perfect woman if only in my mind.

*This is how I see my wife for it is with her I am even a better
man than the Lord has made. Combined with her soul, I
feel there is nothing I cannot accomplish. That can only be
done by submitting ones life to the Lord and trusting that
what He gives back is a perfect you, regardless of what
others think and feel.*

HARMONY

The idea that I am your equal scares me.
Thoughts that we must share this existence together have
fled.
At times, I've forgotten that connection and misplaced my
soul.
I have ventured away from the bond that made us
complete.

But,

The coming of a new day begins when I find my way back
to your side.
I am truly a man only when my Woman is reconnected to
my being.
The world will right itself when our union is complete.
I am truly defined by the Woman I share this earthly plane
with.

But,

True happiness comes when I have an equal and our spirits
are fused.
This is the master plan forgotten.

The universe will align and cosmic order will be restored.
When these wrongs are righted God will smile on us.

But,

I am less than what I can be and will be without you
We've been connected from the beginning of time.
The way to salvation is the road traveled with you.
God laid the foundation for our future; it's that union we
    share.

THAT SMILE

All you did was invite me in with that smile and I wonder
can I hold up.

The essence of your body and soul captivate and sedate me.

I am powerless from the notion of being in your thoughts;
it has moved me to heights never reached in all my
dreams.

The feeling of your glance is like the warmth from a sunlit
summer morning.

We have bonded and you haven't even touched me.

The tranquil serenity of your voice caresses my heart.

My words get tangled when attempting to utter your name
to others who will listen to my babbling.

How did I become this lucky to have you and be accepted
into your space?

Who knew a momentary look could shake a person's soul
and spirit.

You are the reason I stand here wanting more of who you
appear to be.

Can I be the man that worships the artwork God has
created; am I truly worthy of sharing a being as
wonderful as you?

Your beauty is a testament to a legacy that was yours long
before you drew a single breath.

Each intense thought firing in my brain sends word
    through my body that God is real.
All you did was invite me in with that smile and I wonder
    can I hold up.

A REAL MAN'S STRENGTH

Listen, a test of a man comes when his pride is touched.
How he holds his tongue and allows the events to play out.
His values are his anchor and morals become his sails.
So deal with hard time, understand you are becoming
    better with each moment.
Hard times befall all who live life.
How you recover measures how hard things truly were.
When tested, the strong soul will survive but change.
This change will heal and protect your swollen or bruised
    pride.
Your prayers will be answered, but these situations are
    God's design for you.

BIG GIRL

Yes, Big Girl, it's you!!
Excuse me miss, may I take your hand and chill with you?
Are you here alone because I don't want to be rude?
Do me the pleasure of making me look real good by your
 side on the dance floor.
Come have a seat and share a drink with me and let me
 learn your story.
Yes, Big Girl, it's you!!
Damn can't wait for her to get here, I hope she likes the
 apartment.
My God, you look great better than the first night I saw
 you.
Kiss me so you can see how much I have wanted you to
 come here and chill with me.
Rest your feet on my couch, I got dinner and something to
 drink, It was white wine right?

Yes, Big Girl, it's you!!
Oh my! Where do I touch first, your body is divine as
 those statues one sees in history books.
Your skin is as soft as a baby and your perfume is driving
 me crazy.

Each roll and the fullness of your body have me excited
and focused at the same time.
I can't wait to hear you make those sexy noises that only a
fully aroused woman makes.

Yes, Big Girl, it's you!!
I would have never imagined that your lips could taste this
sweet let me handle the rest.
Your ample breasts are the reason men question their
prowess. You have them wondering if they can please
you.
As I reach your second lips, I am taken by the fact you
have allowed me this pleasure.
It's as if nectar runs from your loins, with each brush of my
tongue.

Yes, Big Girl, it's you!!
Your body seems ready; I can't get anymore excited I must
what I have craved since I met you.
The heat is staggering I have to close my eyes to make it
pass the feeling of release.
Your full frame seems to welcome me closer as you wrap
around me and we become one.
My manhood is accepted and I feel that you have been
what I have longed for.

Yes, Big Girl, it's you!!

With each stroke, my being and soul are bonding with
yours.

With each passing moment, I am drawn closer and closer
to that moment when you will have me.

You have expressed your delight with the series of moans
that come from your mouth like song.

My breathing begins to change and you demand I look at
you.

Yes, Big Girl, it's you!!

My hands grip your body, mine tightens, and our eyes are
locked.

Damn, the emotions are overwhelming as my mouth flies
open at the same moment I release.

My juices take flight filling your center with all that makes
me a man, mixing with the juices that make you a
woman.

My eyes have never left yours, as my body shivers with
each sec.

Yes, Big Girl, it's you!!

You continue to move your body as if you we're winding
down an exercise routine.

Your hands touch my face to console me.

Wiping away the sweat from my chin and brow, your smile
of satisfaction has me, as I collapse onto that full figure

of yours into those loving arms and as this dream comes
to an end, I utter
Yes, Big Girl, it's you!!

MY GHETTO GIRL!!

No, I don't want to tap That, Stick That, Lick that or Split
   That
But I do want to Hug You, Love You, Please You and Place
   No One above You.

No, I don't want a Ride or Die Chick, a Down With it
   *itch, a hocchie Queen, Chicken Head or Bird.
But I do want a B-U-D-D-Y, a Nina to my Darius, a
   Monica to my Quincy or a Corretta to my Martin.

No, I don't want you to Hold the Heat, Rock the Whip all
   while counting your Lootchie playing with your
   Coochie.
But I do want that Superwoman, who can keep a home,
   hold her own, who rocks me to sleep with loving so
   good, at times I can't speak.

No, I don't want to sneak, creep, pimp, prowl, or cheat
   with you and your peeps.
But I want to be a one-woman man, who takes you out so
   the world can see my blessing and the Lord in your
eyes.

No, I don't want to be your Maintenance Man, Your
    Service Dude, Mr. Right Now, or Your Late night come
    by when the kids are sleep and be gone before they
    wake Man.
But I do want to be the come over and make dinner, invite
    your children to chill with mine, no living at home with
    my mother or too many baby mamas who call all times
    of night type of guy.

No, I don't want be that hell yea I'll leave if the stick is
    blue, family asking, *"So Now What You Going to Do?"*
Fellas mumbling, *"Make Sure it's you?"*
I want to marry you because I Love You. Not because of
    our seed, I'll take care all its needs. So wipe your tears,
    it's a moment to be shared. For it is to you I swear,
My Ghetto Girl!

GIVE IN

Your rhythmic movements have sent a strong message to
   my body
I am trying to hold on and hold out, trying not to end this
   moment too soon
Your movement is slow, deliberate, controlled and
   passionate. I am in erotic bliss
Your whispers are like thunder as your voice surrounds my
   mind

Your skin is silky smooth and your touch is artistically
   simplistic
I bite my lip to gain a hold of what should be my moment
I have never been blessed with such a loving partner
I can sense that feeling drawing close, your eyes lock in

As I try to turn the tables, to take control, it is quickly
   taken back
You are like the petals of flowers, sexy looking and soft to
   the touch
My mind is a blaze but you demand my attention, I am
   powerless
How can I continue at this pace, was this your plan, to
   break me?

K. L.

Didn't I ask for this when I said be mine, didn't I want this
    when I said let's do this?
My body can't resist you any longer; I have to let go, but
    what about you
The pace quickens; you know you have me don't you
My heart speeds up, my teeth are clinched and the last
    thing I can remember hearing is your voice sweetly
saying,

GIVE IN

JUST WONDERING
Peaking into a man's mind

Have you sat and thought about why you are here? I have. I know it sounds corny or redundant, but nonetheless it's a valid question. I ask this of myself when I consider my actions towards others and the feelings I have before, during and after a relationship, or the potential of one. First, let me introduce myself to you.

Hello, I am a liar, a cheat a façade of a man. I am not always the strong together person I seem to be. Many nights I am a fearful child who cling to things the way one does to its mother. I am not the smooth operator that strides as he walks but more a boy who wants to blend in and tries not to be picked on or seen. I will tell you tales of wonderment of places I have been and things I have seen, only to blind you to the things I have not accomplished with myself or places I have only dreamt of going to. I am not the one-woman man I say I am but more of a greedy woman monger who wants all I can bed down. I am not the well off person I say I am. I have more bills then I can pay. I am not the independent, self-sufficient Hercules, but more of a living-at-home hope to be mortal.

Then there are the days I wonder from a different point of view. I wonder about things that would make me a real man. I think about how to be more of what I would like to be instead of what I am not at the moment. Let me introduce myself to you.

Hello, I was a hurting sad male, who has lifted himself up from the floor only to try things again. I didn't know how to manage without the help of a woman. Now, I am willing to work twice as hard to make a good woman smile with what I have. Yes, these are my Sunday and my party clothes, just different shoes. You don't have to worry. I will keep them clean. I'll never wear the same thing the next day after I have spent the night dancing and sweating with you. No, I don't drive a fancy car like many that have it that way, but I'll keep this one running and anything else I work on in the house. I once desired the feeling of having many different women around me for what they can bring to my bed. But now, I am smart enough to know that one special woman is worth all of the others wrapped up and then some.

When I used to look out the window, I dreamed of all the places I couldn't go. Now, I work both of these jobs because I understand that someday I will travel when and where I want. Church was never my thing; it started too early and ended too late. Now, I understand everything starts with God and He is the only one who can lead me to what I was meant to be.

The answers to everything I am are not clear. To me, there are things I know I am and things I know I am not. The only way for you to find out who I am, is to take the time and risk the pleasure or pain to learn as I do. Let me say Thank You, or I'm Sorry before we go any farther. I am still not sure which person you will find in me or which person I have been to you. Forgive me, I was just sitting here wondering why I am.

WHY DID I TELL THOSE LIES?
The other side of men you don't see.

Why did I tell those lies??

I should have told you, hell no, they aren't all my friends, just conquests I haven't gotten to yet.

I wanted you to chase after me when I walked out of the club when you asked me about that woman.

I am scared and don't trust myself, that's why I call you so much.

I wanted a mother, lover and baby moms too look after me.

I look at other women to make myself feel more important.

I get angry at the next guy because my game is not tight.

I am not going to pay back the money that I borrowed to go out with the next chick.

I still don't get this monogamy thing because I didn't try understanding what you needed.

I really did think I'm sorry and a sad face could heal this.

I want each chick on my web page to think they are special; it helps me get to the panties.

However,

I have matured spiritually, mentally and emotionally since
  our last fall out.
I have to learn to call before I come over.
I will stand with you in church and get the word I need to
  be a better man.
I wont flip when another man post a slick remark on your
  web page.
I need you more than the damn Lakers.
I agree there are times I need to act grown up. Today is a
  great day.
I know it's time to put up or shut up and become your
  equal, your protector and possibly your best friend.
I am done with multiple women and it's you I want.
I am no longer scared of admitting I need the Lord and
  your love.
I only pray that it's not too late to repair what I have done.
I laugh as my boys ask, "Why the sad face, are you missing
  your woman?"
I say, "Man, I am cool as a fan," but my heart and soul
  screams out
Why did I Tell Those Lies??

WHO ARE YOU?

With the moon light from the window shining down on
   me I ask myself, who are you?
Thinking I had it all with you beside me, I never thought
   about, who are you?
From the pleasure of each movement of our bodies as we
   made love it never dawned on me, who are you?
You were there for me when others did me wrong so did I
   ask, who are you?
As the love grew to levels many dream of I never
   questioned, who are you?
But as things started to pop up, I didn't think about, who
   are you? With each new screen name, I didn't worry
   about, who are you?
With each coincidence, I didn't have to ask, who are you?
Now as my heart sits broken I wonder all this time, who
   are you? Wondering why you're not here me or me with
   you I still don't know, who are you?
Now the pain is here and won't go away all because I didn't
   find out, whom are you?
We discussed what my fears were and talked about yours,
   how is I still don't know, who are you?
There were things that I asked and needed too know but
   one I surely knew was who are you?

I thought I was clear and you heard every word but to
    think I really don't know who are you?
If this love was real, I should never have had to ask, who
    are you? Why have you kept me out, not let me in,
    what a thing to do to someone who said I love you too,
    but with all that has happen I am still left asking,
Who are you?

K. L.

HAPPY OR NOT VALENTINE'S DAY!!!

It is the time of the year again, the time that lovers and
haters live for.
Many will spend a moment emotional over the gifts
bought, made, or delivered.
The others will gripe, complain, argue with all who will
listen about things so absent too them.

As the day begins, many are reminded of their love-ones
current, past, good and bad.
As the others spend the day marveling, reminiscing,
disliking, or hating and it's okay.
This day is for that.

It's a day to help you love stronger or push you farther over
the cliff of self-pity.
Your PC, DVD, CD, VCR, Radio, and TV will be used as
tools of sensitivity or weapons of self-pity.
As the night comes to a close, it will be filled with the
sounds of love or the scowls of despair.

Many a bed will be a playground of affection or a pit of
anguish.
Dreams will be filled with the content feelings only love
brings or the contempt the absences of it creates.

48

But it is okay. It is that time of the year again.
Happy or Not Valentine's Day!!

K. L.

NOW WHO WILL HOLD ME?

As the night rolls to an end
I have lost a friend
As my heart tries to mend
With no love left to lend
As the pain sets in
The way I feel must be a sin
I lay back and start to cry
As part of me starts to die
Alone is how I'll stay
So tonight, I pray
Which I hope is the key
And, I ask quietly to myself,
Now who will hold me?

PAIN

Some can argue but I know pain is needed.
We can't grow and become what we will without enduring
   pain.
Our first breath came at the expense of our mother's pain
Pain is present at every turn as a reminder of our human
   limits.
Some thrive on causing others immense pain.
We try shielding ourselves from the affects and causes of
   pain.
Pain makes us stronger, wiser and more respectful.
Our children, our elderly are more open to receive pain.
We aspire to great heights when we realize how to block
   out or forget about pain.
We reconnect with family, friends, loved ones and even
   ourselves when overcoming pain.
Each person has their own but we all share the same
   reactions, feelings, and tears from pain.
I can't remove yours only help you see what I see, because I
   may be the cause of some of your pain.
I am reaching back my hand to help you because to help
   you I have to let my own pain go.
There will come a time when we feel no more pain.
Until then we have to hope we live the lives we were
   supposed to in spite of pain.

However, God gave pain to us to show us why we will always need him.

UNTIL

The funny thing is you never expected it to happen like this. You didn't believe that a person could slide pass your defenses and touch your soul. You began to live, enjoy and love them. You hated to even say good-bye so you utter the word UNTIL.

It left you with the hope and joy that you would be connected like this again very soon. It's funny that the smell of a certain perfume and the touch of someone's hands can alter your existence. But a good part of your life has been spent running from these feelings scared to let another in. Always reminded of the pain the last person made you feel when you allowed them closer. But when you parted, it was always UNTIL.

The lovemaking had taken on newness each time; your mind was blown on the fact someone had mastered your body, your feelings, your being. Stop! This can't be real. This has to be a lie, are you that scared to commit to what you're feeling. You swore you would never let another get this close to the real you. How did they do it? How did they get past the cynical you, the doubting you the hurting you? How did they make you want more of the very thing you were afraid of? So, you leave each time with a simple kiss and the word UNTIL flows from your lips.

K. L.

Each time you meet, it's like the start of this beautiful relationship all over, how? When did God make a person who can connect to all your ports and leave an intelligent person like yourself with nothing but guesses as answers? But you're hooked! Even your breakups don't hurt because you know that they're not permanent. You know they have your soul and you will come back to claim it, even when someone else has stepped in to share your mind and body. It's not complete because its not you or so you think! As you walk around feeling empty, you're reminded of that one word, UNTIL.

Then it hits you like the way Tyson use to fight before he himself had his downfall, you weren't being true the whole time so the words were tainted that came from you. You realize it's really over and you have lost a great LOVER, PARTNER, BUDDY, and FRIEND. The thoughts sink deep and reach those places that you are scared to face, the places only a mirror reaches; the places where only your dreams and fears live, the places where only you take yourself on certain occasions.

This happens to be one of those occasions. It becomes clear, what you have done to yourself and you're faced with the understanding that you hoped you would never find. The meanings to UNTIL as they spoke it, was simple; UNTIL meant, *"YES, BABY, I GOT YOU, UP TO THIS POINT. AFTER THIS POINT, YOU HAVE TO FACE AND DEAL WITH THE WORLD ALONE! MY LOVE COULDN'T*

SAVE YOU FROM YOUR OWN DEMONS!"

But you couldn't see what they meant when they said it. Like you said to yourself at the jump, you never expected it to happen like this. No one ever does, UNTIL.

Dedicated to all those that mislead others only to find they found and lost a part of themselves they never knew!

K. L.

ONE WORD

There are no words to explain,
the feeling of joy you filled my heart with or the pain that
has replaced it.
There are no words to explain,
What sharing each other's body felt like or what being
alone does to a man.
There are no words to explain,
The look on your face as our hands and minds intertwined
but now I wrap myself in sadness to get to sleep.
There are no words to explain,
The time quickly passed when we sat and talked compare
to how long the days run with my own thoughts.
There are no words to explain,
The warmth I was filled with to watch you smile but now
my frown is a constant reminder.
There are no words to explain,
The completeness of having had someone like you in my
life to knowing that by myself is where I'll stay.
There are no words to explain,
Because there is one word that explains it all good or bad,
happy or sad;
"LOVE"

MY GODDESS

How do you calm a raging fire, you find a way to douse the flames from all angles. The pains I have, seems to become calm when talking to my Goddess.

How do you help a person with a deathly fear, you slowly show them there is nothing to fear by placing yourself in it's path and act like a bridge for that person to walk across?

The fears I have, my Goddess you have reached out and extended yourself as a buffer from the pain I hold.

How do you teach someone to trust again, you show them that there is nothing hidden when talking to them?

My issues with trust, my Goddess you ask me to let go, so that you can hold and heal my tattered heart.

How do you find the Lord when you have wondered around blindly, you drop to your knees and ask that Lord show you the way home again and let him plant the pathway in you heart and mind?

My Goddess you have crossed my path and now you walk alongside of me, at the same time asking to help me with directions to things since lost.

How do you recover from a mistake of epic proportions, You lift yourself up and fight to get back in the game as if there is no tomorrow and remain focused on the what will be, not the what has been. The errors I have made and the pain they caused, my Goddess you asked to step in and fight this fight along side of me and when need be in front of me. Your light re-ignites my own.

How do you know whom to choose when faced with many who want you, you close your eyes and let your heart guide your actions

As I live this life, I am told what could be done to me and for me by so many, but you my Goddess say, "I am what you need me to be."

So my Goddess I offer this. Allow me to move as the mortal I am. Learn as the mortal I am. Enjoy the gift as the mortal man I am. This will allow me to grow to become the god that is needed by you my goddess

MY PROPSAL

Here is an actual fantasy. The night before Valentine's Day, we arrived in Mexico, somewhere along the Mayan Riviera. We spent the night in a romantic cabin with nothing modern to work with. The next morning there is fresh squeezed juice and sliced fruits waiting at your side of the bed. I nudge you oh so gentle to awake.

After bathing under fresh spring water in a hand made shower we walk along the beach, which is just to the back of the cabin. The beach is ours for the next couple of miles. As we sit to relax, we fall in love all over again listening to stories long forgotten about each other. These were the things we found endearing to begin with. We make love knowing we are all alone.

Resting on the beach we lay back to allow the nice warm tropical breeze blow across our bodies. I take you to the cabin I have something for you. Unknown to you, people from the main land came in and set our place up for a candle lit dinner. Seven Courses and wine chilled on ice. As the sun rolls away and we have finished a wonderful meal.

We stand at the rear of the cabin and look at the waves and listen to what only the Lord has put into place. As we fall deeply in to the seen of great tranquility, I reach into my pocket and lower my self to one knee and look you into those beautiful eyes and say "Make my world complete? Be the one who I start and end my day with until the day the Lord calls me home.

WOULD YOU PLEASE DO ME THE HONOR OF BECOMING MY WIFE?"
All this happens on FEB 14 of the Year?
Like I said it's a fantasy.

I am married now and if I could go back and ask Tiffany all over again, this is how I would have done it.

CHAPTER 3

Fatherhood.

These are the words that rise up and out of Father, Son and Husband trying to be the Man for his family.

As a father, you learn that the world is not perfect and neither are you. It will become clear with each day on this planet that all relationships require hard work. These words have come from the life experience of man trying to make a difference in the lives of those close to him.

These poems came about when I sat down and realized that I am someone's father. Growing up, like many young men, I didn't know my father. The Lord allowed my father and me to reconnect after thirty-nine years. The Lord allowed us to finally meet two weeks before my wedding. When I write I don't know where it's going to go. With this subject there are so many mixed emotions however, I can only tell you that it's all from the heart. You just don't know what feelings are going to come to the forefront. You don't know how much of yourself you're going to actually allow to be seen. Being a parent is a very special circumstance. It's also one of the areas that are so sadly overlooked when young men go out and create children. I know. I was one of those young men who went out and created life I couldn't and didn't take care of.

Being the parent of four children, with three different women, some could really say I was ultra irresponsible. I was. Regardless of the circumstance, the children are here and I'm making a strong attempt to be a stand up father. It's not easy, there is a lot of damage to try to repair, but the moments that you have to spend time with them is nonetheless special. The moment that you look at them, watch them, and listen to them, something inside you changes. It hurts and touches you at the same time. It's the strangest feeling. Loving and disliking a moment all at the same time. if young men would stop and really consider what the role of a father is, I don't think they would go out and make children so randomly like they are doing. As you read this particular section, understand that this is just how I see my role as a father. It's not a perfect role, and I think I tried to capture that in some of the words that I have here. One of my favorites in this section is **I'm Not Superman, I'm Dad**. I think too often we try to become superman and we can't. Too many get caught up in trying to be a superhero and stop being Dad. The fear of failing will cause many of us to never step up to the plate and become just that, Dad. I think this is a revealing section and I hope that you enjoy it.

I LOVE YOU QUEEN

The essence of what I am started deep inside of you when
the Lord set me in place.
Your choice to have me was the first of many that would
lead my steps
Those late night talks and listening to you pray for me
touched me inside you long before I could see you to
return the favor.

My suckling was our period of bonding, who knew it was
healing you.
My cries were soothed with the beating of your heart along
with the soft notes of song from your lips.
The constant encouragement to venture on my own made
me brave enough to step and fall, but I learned.
Now its outside and a new fear begins, but your teaching
was clear as I make friends, smiling as I have been
taught.

You say go ahead, I'll be here at the end of the day, my
world is shaken but I hear, this is growth, and education
shouldn't be feared is whispered in my ear.
With each cap and gown and picture day I am becoming a
man, because of the woman you are.

K. L.

My legs stretch and my arms lengthen, my face eases past
  yours as now I look down at the center of my universe.

My mind is confused and my body feels stranger, you have
  the answers my manly eyes are opening.
You point out class is internal and trash is external so I
  understand what you meant when you said Self Respect
  is not an option.
Your face frowns as you look her over, you feel challenged
  but she is not and will not be you. I am growing and
  you got me here for a reason.

Now I stand proud and humble, the Lord smiles at the job
  you've done.
I have blessed this world with heirs and you are the roots of
  our tree.
My feelings for you are still the same as that little boy
  who you didn't help who fell and cried out for you, now
  this man understands why you didn't run to pick him,
  for doing so I say to you,
I LOVE YOU QUEEN

*Dedicated to my mother and all the sisters trying to raise
boys into men. You're not forgotten. We love you and don't
give up. We will turn into the men you dreamed us to be.*

THE BIRTH
One of the days my life changed forever

Today I have seen God at work.

I was reminded of how powerful the lord really is. Let me walk you through what I'm talking about. Over nine months ago our union began. Our intertwined bodies were sealed from our lips to our hips. We were one. My holders of life, met your seeds of creation, we were complete.

Over the first three months, I watched you change. I changed along with you. Your body swells and the life we created grows. You are so beautiful to me, my queen. As the next three months pass, we are taken to another plateau. We are at the point where it's too far to look back and not close enough to the end. Your hands and feet are swollen. Your smile is missing. What do I do? I rub your head and hold your belly. I say don't worry lover, "This to shall pass." The last three months brings us to the final lap. I see your discomfort but it is mixed with joy. Each kick of out future excites us. We decided not to find out the gender of our child, we believe that it's the way God intended it. As you sleep, I can't. The excitement of being a father and husband is at times overwhelming. The days are beginning to drag. Our child has made the turn to head downward in your stomach. I am so amazed at how you deal with all this. I am gaining a new respect for you and every woman that has gone through this journey.

Then the day comes. Your cries from another part of the house pierce my ears like the scream of the Banshee. We are in flight, with the wheel in one hand, the cell phone in the other, one eye on traffic, and another one on you. I get us to the hospital with the quickness of racecar driver. Like VIP's at the latest club, we zip right through, on to the birthing room. Your gown is in place; your hair is tied back (like we agree). We are ready. As the doctors slide into place, they field their position like a well-coached sports team.

As we learned in Lamaze class to stay focused and listen to the doctors. Now the fear sets in inside me. What if something goes wrong, like in the movies? Things start to look strange to me. The room is closing in on me. I am feeling lost and scared. As if you could read my mind, you reach out and hold my hand, saying, "You're doing fine, baby." How about that in the mist of that is happening, you reach to calm me down. Can I love you anymore than I do right now? The doctor summons me to the head of the bed. He instructs me to watch.

Then it happens. God's will and his work are revealed to me. I watch this small life appear, fighting its' way into this world. I am witnessing time and space beginning to slip into to separate realms. Then it happens, the arrival. It's a boy, but I don't hear anything, no sounds. My heart stops and my fears have returned. However, like earlier something is done to calm me and it's our child's screams of life. The soft but strong screams of this little prince sound like music. He calms and warms my soul. I count his fingers and toes as my great-grandmother told me years ago to do.

I hold him close to you and kiss you and him. I am the luckiest man on the planet. God has truly blessed me. I smile proudly as my tears fall down my checks.

Today I have seen God at work.

With witnessing the birth of my sons, I would never be the same. The blocks were beginning to lie in place. I was slowing moving on to the path of being a father. If only I had listened to that voice than. God speaks softly but if you miss it, there are powerful ramifications to your life. Give him a chance to work and you see. I seen his work but missed his voice

MY CHILDREN
A Personal Haiku

Be better than I was
Eclipse my successes
push to edge pass my goals
Learn more than I have ever dreamed of.
Love stronger than I, hurt and suffer less.

MY CHILDREN

Live for today and plan for tomorrow
Protect yourself from those that take
Forgive me if you are unable
Praise me if your capable

MY CHILDREN

The Devil May Have I
Pray God Will Spare Me,

MY CHILDREN

I May Not be Superman, but I'm Dad

I am flawed, not perfect, my strength is normal, but my
heart is big.
I haven't been to every match, game or event. My soul was
there when I thought of your performance. I did love
your mother then, but parenting doesn't require a loving
union, just a respectful one.
I may not be Superman but I'm Dad

As you grow discontent, confusion, anger and despair
might try to set in. My arms, eyes, and ears are open
and I am here for you when you're ready. The Cosby's
are real and you could become Theo or Vanessa.
However, I am not Cliff Huxtable so our problems won't
end in an hour with a poignant lecture and a smile.
I may not be Superman but I'm Dad

You're neither the only one I have nor the only one I love.
But, I had no one to show me or tell me a father is more
then a bedfellow. Your desires are big and your dreams
even bigger. My prayers are greater then both since I
know who and what I don't want you to become.
I may not be Superman but I'm Dad

K. L.

You will hear so much about me from so many sources.
Our time together should heal some of the wounds they
    open and keep open.
Leave your faith in GOD; He blessed you with life. I pray
    one day we'll sit and I'll try to explain that:
I may not be Superman but I'm Dad

*Every father in the world has to simply try their best to
just be themselves. Not a superhero. Their children will
make them that on their own. I lost so much creating
lives I couldn't take care of at the same time. I beg every
man that reads this poem. If you have life in your body,
then there is still time to change your situation with
your kids and become their hero. It's greater to have
heard them say, "I love you," one day than go a lifetime
wondering if they did.*

YOUNG CHILD
Teenage Pain

With each scream and curse, you speak a clear language
    that only a parent can hear.
Your friends are oblivious to its critical message that spells
    out the pain you suffer.
Reacting like a wounded animal, you lash out at all who
    try to save you.
The circle of wondering eyes are made up of the same
    structure and pain filled souls.
Each feeding on the other's anger and pain not knowing
    the overflow of emotion is pure poison.
Absence is the power of the fear we have tried to instill in
    you.
Together you all find strength, comfort, companionship
    and even belonging.
However, in each one of you there is emptiness, the
    missing of smiles, hugs, laughter and true Love of self.
When others try to penetrate the circle, you form an
    impregnable wall, a force to be reckoned with.
With each moment, the power surge, the feelings of
    superiority swells, and gas is poured onto an internal
    fire.
All that is missing is the match.

You crave for someone to make the mistake of thinking
    they can walk the path through this levy of misguided
    youth.
Safety in numbers is displayed in each handshake, hug and
    well wish.
We see the truth, each embrace is a cry for safety, each hug
    is reassuring touch and each word is gesture of comfort.
But, it's at this moment the seed, which was placed deep in
    you, begs to be open, needing good soil to cling too.
All that is missing is the water of faith, the fertilizer of a
    home filled with compassion and grace.
Inside you will grow justice, righteousness and Love
Why do we push and cling so hard you ask.
We know with each moment away from the collective you
    grow and mature into that being that we dreamt of.
We try to convince you that time is the missing element
    that will produce the great things we promised.
Our tears attempt to pierce your harden shell and its here
    we draw the line in the sand.
US OR THEM!

So, choose your path wisely and understand that pressure is
    not applied but accepted.
As you return as part of the anti-society you created,
    remember, true Love doesn't come with limits, demands
    or a price other then mutual trust.

Make each step count for as you move you are changing
and it may become permanent.

Say goodbye to innocents for the serpent has gotten past
your mental perimeter.

Choose wisely child, I'll hold this place in my heart open
for you if you make it back.

Take the only thing I know to be greater then that energy
you young ones feed off, the open gracious arms of the
one who knows all.

*Dedicated to my daughter and other teenagers who are
feeling confused, forgotten or just left out. I understand
your pain but I can't hold your hand when you walk out
the door. All I can send with you is my guidance, my love
and my prayers. All the choices after that are yours.*

K. L.

THE SMILES NOT SEEN, THE CRIES NOT HEARD
The Abortion Poem

As the seeds depart and searches for their assigned meeting
place, the journey commences.

There are millions in tow, and only one will have the right
to connect with the gracious host.

The womb has prepared a lovely reception for a welcomed
guest.

Then the magic happens, God's finger touches the cradle of
life, two become one.

Each day the gift grows, filled with the joy of the moment
and the promise of a bright future.

But alas,

All the love you feel may not be enough to change the
outcome.

The body is a mystery regardless of what the doctors know
they are powerless.

You're faced with the truth, the struggle begins, the test, or
maybe even the devil is at play.

It's now clear, the magic won't happen, the candle is out,
and God has spoken.

For you, all that's left is to sit quietly, pray, weep and dream
about;

The smiles not seen and the cries not heard!

Dedicated to all who face that choice, made that choice, had no choice, or that choice was made for you.

K. L.

THE DEVIL IS SMILING

Men don't see it or hear it but the message is loud.
Women struggle with pain, their joy is gone.
Our children act unaware and don't know.

In groups, we stalk and alone we are worse.
Our ladies bear all, in attempts to be loved.
The children mirror what they've been taught.

We spend money to hide the dirty deed left behind only to
sin some more.
The cultivators of life destroy the tracks and cover up the
traces of our evil deeds.
But, the seeds push through and grow, showing battle scars
from a war they didn't start.

The Y chromosome demands his fill; he was taught this is
the way to do things.
The X chromosome lies in place as this union of filth is
played out in her womb.
The combination succeeds; the product is doomed to begin
the journey once again.

In the later day's, age, time, and an inner spirit springs
forth and cries out loud.
The vision of beauty has soon departed and the grim
reminder of holy promise fades away.
The evolution has taken placed and the baton is passed, the
cycle is in motion only to repeat itself.

All, while the Devil smiles!

*Men sometimes we forget how connected we are to our
women and our children. As we go so do they. The Lord
didn't want us estrange from our holy partners. Men it
starts with us. When I come into school each day and
see how our children act, it makes me wonder what is
happening behind the scenes. The devil must really be
having fun with all this mess.*

DIVORCE

Didn't our vows mean you'll love me and I'll love you?
Weren't we supposed to be a team?
To grow old together so it seemed.

The Oath was until death do us part.
Didn't the vows go *"DO YOU"* at the start?
Damn how did we get here?
You live there and I live nowhere near.

How did all the time go by and we not get close?
Wasn't our marriage stronger than most?
Was it being young or the pressure at that time?
Or did we both realize we were not in our right minds.

I thought I knew love and all that came with it
But to have a great marriage there is work that goes in it.
I may sound silly and maybe naive
I didn't know my ex had so many pet peeves.

So I look back and instead of happy I see sad.
You don't get married to turn out mad.
The outcome wasn't one sided, I helped in this demise
I wasn't a married man, but a man in a marriage. Isn't that
    a surprise?

Now my focus is on my future and now a days that's the
    trend
All you really lose when you're divorced is the trust,
    support and love of a friend.

***If you have ever been married and faced a divorce, you'll
understand where my heart was. Who stands there on
that day to end up in a bad way?***

IT JUST HIT ME

We have moved in totally opposite directions and decided
to go on and live our lives.
We are mere images of a time since past. Now the only
thing left is to find a way to be respectful in our strive

We are only parents nothing more, with the only respected
constant, our children
We have become one of those couples

We have lost the essences of what many live for, fight for,
die for and cry for
We have place others closer to our hearts and accepted the
fact it is dead

We are now reduced to ex wife and ex husband.
We have as much in common as a Reebok and Nike
sneaker

We have decided another man will be the King in your life
We have decided another sister will be the Queen to
support and treat me nice

We have moved on and decided a death is the outcome of
our union

A Man in Transition

We didn't even have a proper funeral for this marriage

We now have to work at being friendly to each other
We don't even speak as if something might come out the
wrong way to one another

We have reduced ourselves back to the very beginning
We have come full circle to the point where we aren't even
friends.

It just hit me!
As I read the final copies of the legal papers,
Damn, it's really over!

HATE

I wasn't raised with it.
I was taught to let it go because it will burn you up.
I was told there is a thin line between it and love.
It can make a man do crazy things.
It has been the object use to commit many a crime.
Many have died because of it.
It is the source of evil.
With all that is known about it, it is still the motivation for
   many
So all I can do is accept that I feel it
Like a dog that has been beaten to often I have to turn on
   it
Find a way to break free from it
My thinking cannot be shaped by it.
My soul is risk if I don't resist it.
All will be lost if I can't conquer it
For if I don't, I will be overcome with it,
Hate.

DON'T PASS ME BY

Through the eyes of the homeless

You gaze at me as if my face has no features; there is a
human underneath all this.

So you're better than me, as if this was my dream when I
skipped to school along side you.

Look deeper, we are not that different, we are only a few
mistakes away from each other.

*

Food has lost its taste. I eat to survive. Can you relate as
you order lunch?

How dare you think I don't have feelings, try laying here
on a cold winter's night?

Get a job you say, how come it's never, "Do you need some
help?" You're quick to tell but not to offer.

*

Abuse comes in many forms, some I allowed and others I
didn't sign up for.

Ever fought for a bed, food, sneakers or your pride, and
then told you're worthless?

Your God may be good to you, but look up at a large dark
sky, in the middle of a cold night, starving, and you'll
question, does He truly exist?

*

83

Well, I have to go, the shelter gives a whole sandwich
today, plus I can see your Latté is getting cold.
Keep me in mind when you say to your children, "Don't
waste, people are starving in Africa." Guess what, we're
really not that far away.
Please pray along with me as I ask that someday you'll stop
and talk to me, since you don't hear me when I scream,
Don't pass me by!!

Just had to list this one a second time.
Sorry for the repeat. Please help the homeless many
didn't ask or figure they would end up where they are!!!
Too often, we walk right pass grown men, women
families as if they're not there. They are there and
wondering why thy have to beg for help. Why do they
have to create a nuisance to help or support? They seem
to target places that require you to spend some money
and we get upset. I wonder why? Food or drink just
doesn't seem to taste the same with hungry eyes on you.

CHAPTER 4

The Educator.
I am a Shaper of Minds and Builder of Dreams. The Hardest
Job you'll ever Love.

As a teacher of today's children, I am faced with so much that the world doesn't see. Their ups and downs, their triumphs and crashes yet you have to press on with the learning. These are just a few words that came from those visions.

I'm a teacher. Is there any greater job on the planet? I wouldn't know. I've been doing this for some time now. Over twelve years to be exact. So, to me, it is the greatest job a person could have because it's never the same. No day is similar to the one before. The setting may be the same but the situations change, and change rapidly. As a teacher, you don't know what you're going to come into a classroom and have to deal with. It's like being on stage; live theater and you don't get a retake. At the end of the day, you have to take that educator's hat off, return back to girlfriend, husband, and brother, whatever. All while waking up in the morning and coming right back on stage. You see these kids start to expect you to be that stage personality everyday. They grow to trust the stage you. They grow to open up and even love you. This is hard for some of these children today. On the bad days, you better not dare show them something that they weren't prepared for. You may lose that child for the rest of his life.

I hope that when you are reading these poems and stories that you get that feeling or understand the frustration that goes through a teacher when he's trying to reach a child and what he has to deal with each day when he says to himself I really want to make a difference. Because there are a few of us still out here.

A Teacher's Prayer

Heavenly Father,
I understand I can't save all of them.
I know I sometimes miss the mark with some.
I must work from sun up to sun down and then again.
Each night I try to come up with a way to touch every soul.
I love when I see the light go on when a child truly understands.
I live for the hugs of the little ones smiling and saying thanks.
I'll find a way to rest and recover after diligently protecting each child.
I am comfortable with the idea of starting this process all over again each year.
I am grateful, that I am one your builders' of minds, shapers' of dreams and cultivators' of the future.
Thank You for Blessing me Father to be a Teacher

Dedicated to every teacher who walks into a classroom wanting to make a difference.

K. L.

I Am Only As Strong As You Allow Me to Be

Each morning the challenge is afoot.
What illusion can I create today?
How do I enhance a future I may not see?

I really do care even if my style seems tough.
I know the world and this is one coat of armor I'll make
     sure you hold on too. They have given me 185 days to
     fuel your dreams.

More homework? Yes everyday! It's to make sure you take
     home the gifts offered in class.
This isn't easy, imagine 22 others like yourself and I have to
     love you all the same.
You hear and see a lesson; I hear and see love, excitement
     and hope.

Your frustrations pokes at my heart, but the joy will follow
     I promise.
Oh, I won't stop no matter how much you pout, hiss, or
     even curse.
You're simply saying "Do you have me if I fail?" I sure do!

But alas the time will come when you'll have to move on.
Don't worry; enjoy the move, your ready.
I have hidden a piece of me inside you.

You'll see the minute you're asked "Were you ever taught
  this?"
Simply smile and say yes! Someone worked with me on
  this.
You see little one that is the whole trick to this game;
I am only as strong as you allow me to be.

K. L.

YOU ASK WHY AM I SO MEAN
A Teacher's response.

Your life is in my hands, but I can't help you now unless
you let me.

They have designed a slow death for you, if you can't make
it.

Without your help I can't stop it. I'll resist as hard as I can
for as long as I can.

I swear to protect you. I have dedicated my life to assisting
you.

The devil hides in the suits and agendas laid out by those
that don't even know you or care.

I'll fight as long as I breathe.

From you I'll only ask a few things; that you stay strong,
stay focused, and trusts that I know what I am doing.

They'll send their assassins; they will look friendly and will
sound concerned. They will tell you they know what is
best for you.

Open your eyes, the third one first. Your ears must become
more sensitive than normal.

Let the drums of our ancestors whisper to your soul.

Together I'll try to get you where you need to go. When
you make it to the land of being grown, remember these
days.

Long after I have moved on, save these days to reach back
  for those that are where you are now.
Do this teacher proud: tell my story to those born from
  your successful passage through time.
Now you have your answer to why I am so mean.

K. L.

A NOTE TO THE STUDENTS
911 Remembered by a Teacher

As you watch the horror and ask your questions, I will try to find the answers to all that you ask.

When you're uncertain and scared, I will be the calm and the rock for you to rest on.

When your world seem like it's closing in on you, I will be the helping hand that holds you.

When you look around and no one is there, I will only be a call away.

If you have lost someone who loves you, I will share with you with the love I have.

When you're thinking you want to quit, I will be the one who nudges you to keep going.

When you say who cares, I will be the one who does.
As you grow and become the man or woman you'll be I'll be here smiling knowing I helped with that growth.

To those students who lost their lives in one foolish act, I will hold a place for you in my heart so you're never forgotten.

To the students I have never met, I will remain this way in case our paths cross.

At a time like this, it is you who makes me remember why I became a teacher.

One of the hardest jobs I will ever love! My Prayers are with you.
This is a note to you the Students

God Bless those children who lost their lives and loved ones!

K. L.

WELCOME HOME

Dedicated to Ms. De Bella, an Art teacher,
who lost her battle to cancer.

Don't be afraid, it was your time.
The time for pain has passed.
Your days of worry are no longer.
I have seen the greatness of your work.

Welcome Home

Your efforts were not in vain; you'll not be forgotten.
The seeds of your wisdom are safely tucked away in your
    students.
Your soul can rest with the knowledge your best was done.
Be at peace.

Welcome Home

Yes heads will lower today, don't worry.
Your artwork will remind them each day of your passion.
The lives you've reached are brighter.
Come rest your head.

Welcome Home

As you see, the stories were true.
So frolic with peace and joy.
Feel no sadness, for others are here to join you in your stay.
This is a place for love and rejoicing.

Welcome Home

To the others left behind, your love will serve as a guide.
When you want, place a loving glance down on the rest of
    your family and friends.
Your talents are needed here.
So from today until forever, rest you have earned it.

***This piece printed in two sections. She meant just that
much to so many children. She put up a great battle
against cancer and many personal problems to continue
to make it to school for the kids. She was truly a
dedicated Educator. She is still missed since 2005.***

K. L.

MY TEACHERS MISSION STATEMENT

In every teacher's life there has to be something you stand for and believe every day you walk into a classroom. Here is mine:

> *"My mission is to help each student develop skills and goals that will make them positive contributors to society. I promise to make learning enjoyable and meaningful each day I walk in a classroom. As an educator, I will offer a "Safe Haven" for any student who wants to learn. I will make every attempt to teach and to use all my abilities to move my students closer to their full positive potential. Each child will be seen as an individual and strong attempts will be made to address every need they have. I pray my students leave my care with the belief that education is the key to accomplishing all their dreams. My students will truly believe someone cares about the person they are and will be."*

This statement will lead me to gain all I want as a teacher because it's a personal guide for me to follow everyday. Plus, I love what I do. As silly as it may sound, I started teaching because I wanted to change the world and be a difference maker. I once had a teacher tell me that I wouldn't amount to anything. I never forgot that.

My mission statement reflects everything I wanted from my teachers when I attended school. I see my classroom as a special place, like I said a "Safe Haven" because I see the lights that appear in the eyes of students when they get an idea or concept. Each student deserves to be protected and nurtured in a positive environment.

My classroom is where I teach social lessons as well as the particular content. I bring articles and artwork that the students are interested in. It gives them an opportunity to connection to the lesson. It's not about teaching for now, but for the future.

This mission is more about who I am then anything else. I hope another teacher feels this way when trying to reach my own children in their classroom. I want my students to grow as men and women, then go out and reach others with something I might have taught them. I push my students to understand their potential and that education is the starting point for the rest of their lives. I pray my students see education as a set of keys to many doors along life's journey. There are many other factors that touch our children. However, the classroom is one of the first places they come, so, why not take advantage of the platform given. There is only limited time to do this before so many other attractions and distractions catch their attention. Many of us never fully reach our maximum potential, but a child still has all the chances to reach theirs. This can only be done with a quality caring strong loving connected and focused teacher. A teacher who understands the super powers they possess in the classroom and the affect they have on this world. I am one of those teachers.

K. L. AKA Mr. B. , "A REAL TEACHER"

CHAPTER 5

Simple Observations of the World.

*With Each Passing Minute, the World Gives Us Situations to
Deal With or Think About; Here is What's Goes
Through My Head.*

I was never one to keep a journal. However, over time
I have collected and held onto a few pieces. Over the
years, I have written things on the internet or to myself
to share my views.

Here in this section, I decided to allow you to see what
goes through my head or what my life has been before,
during or after making changes. Please take a minute to
walk alongside me as I ask questions, make observations, or
just consider the world through my eyes and experiences.

You can't have change, and the essence of that change not
have this world in view. This section is simply a collection
of my observations of this place we call earth. Seeing how
things are going in this world it has to touch you one way or
the other. You can be motivated to make a difference while
you are here or just go along with the daily rotation. Not
really making a mark or having your voice heard, We all

have our fights or struggles, I think that is what I was trying to show with my writing here. My goal was to share my adversities so that maybe I could motivate someone to make a change. I think as a writer, I was nervous about exposing my feelings and being open to public opinion. I think it's in those alone times that we have our strongest epiphanies. It is because we really have a chance to sit quietly and let the Lord speak to us, and all of a sudden so much rushes in there and becomes overwhelming and there it is. That's when we are awakened and all of a sudden, either fear or whatever comes over us, but that's the time, God spoke to me in a conversation and my spirit was touched with the idea that it's okay to contemplate because somebody else is going through the same thing. Knowing someone else has sat there and wanted to be where I am or was where I was and reacted the same way and went on to do whatever they went to do is motivation. And so, I felt that it was time to open this page to the book

A GOOD WOMAN AND A GOOD PLATE OF FOOD

Have you ever noticed that a good woman and a good plate of food makes you feel great? Think about it. I am talking about a good plate of soul food. I mean real soul food. I am talking about the kind of food that touches your mind and body the same as a good woman in your life can.

When hearing her call your name sends feelings through you. Something about looking at some fresh collard greens, rice and peas, macaroni and cheese, roasted turkey with gravy, fried chicken, a fresh roast beef, macaroni or potato salad, candied yams, and, of course, cheesecake or peach cobbler, all the things that make your mouth water. Well stop me if I am wrong, but looking at your woman when she first gets out the shower, walks past you wrapped in a towel, sits and oils her legs, then sliding into whatever she is going to wear that night, hair done, and her nails and toes are done, causes you to react the same way. All of that just jumps out at you and makes your mouth react the same as the plate of food.

Then there is the sweet aroma. Like when you walk into the house and the smell of good cooked food starts to play tricks with your head. It makes you head straight for the kitchen to ask, "What smells so good in here?" Well think about this, it's that same when your woman walks up to hug you and she is wearing a scent that grabs your senses and makes you want to whisk her to the bedroom and ask, "What are you wearing that smells so good?" I know it may seem crazy but stop the next time you're with a good woman and think of how she makes you feel. Then remember when you're sitting down about to eat a meal that you love and see if you don't spot some of the same feelings popping up.

To end this little note, put on some good listening music with your woman and see if things don't get started. Then, when you're about to eat that great plate of soul food or whatever may be to your liking, play that same music and see if the music doesn't enhance the meal the same as it did when you were with your lady.

Before criticizing me for being crazy, give it a thought and let it sink in. Fellas stop and think about it for a minute and ladies ask that man does he agree, or just watch him look at you and then the food and see if it doesn't seem vaguely familiar. Wow, I am hungry now but I am not sure for which one. If I am lucky, I might get both. We will see.

SEX VS. LOVE

Is that what this is all about, SEX! Have we reached a place as humans that sex drives all that we want and all that we do? When I was an erotic writer, I loved to express my thoughts about sex in all forms. But, what happened to the other pleasures in life? What happened to love, and enjoying life for the natural aspects of it? When did love take a back seat to sex? I look around and people are scared to say, "I love you," and mean it. But the same folks will quickly say I want to **** you and your friend. I have damn near lost everything from wanting to have sex instead of looking for love. Something has to change with this. I mean I love sex as much as the next man. But, at what cost does sex touch our souls over being loved? Doesn't love reach out to us in ways sex could never even touch? I rant about this because as humans I think we are lowering the bar instead of raising it. I mean what are we teaching our kids, hell what are we teaching ourselves? There has to be a way to get back to finding more from our partners than the physical or has it always been this way? I just don't get it? Is it fear, blindness, disconcert or just choice?? Who really knows?

Strange Days!

The year 2004 ended with the Tsunami estimating over one hundred thousand dead across multiple countries, August 2005 we witnessed the tragedy of Hurricane Katrina claiming close to two thousand lives, and in October 2005 an estimated seventy thousand people lost their lives in South Asia due to an earthquake. Thousands of people were swept away no longer to be seen in a sudden moment of time. Why is everyone so calm with this or is it just me? I am not one for paranoia but things happen for a reason as my grandmother has said to me often... The lord doesn't collect all these souls for no reason. But, is it the Lord or are these the days the devil has waited on? I mean things are happening in ways I have never seen them.. I have never been the strongest church going person but my love of the Lord has never wavered... These days are scary. I am going to pray a little more, read a little more and try to get right a little more... Something is at work here and even if you just believe in science there still are no true answers to the number of lives that have been lost. What ever your move is today, take a minute to sit quietly and listen to what your inner voice says to you, mine is crying and sounding fearful of what is going on around us. I see our children acting in ways that don't seem right or even natural; parents are losing even more control. Can all this be by accident? I don't know what can be done one way or the other. But, I am going to pray even harder to reach inside myself to be a better teacher, father and husband. I'll try to open the doors to anyone of those children that want to know more about things that are happening in their own worlds. I wanted to put this on the table since death touches all of us in many ways. I came on the internet today only to learn that a friend from the net was called home unexpectedly and here I had chatted with them not to long ago. I open my mail and find another friend has gone home too... What is really going on in the world? Will this touch us any more then it has, like KATIRNA, RITA and any other disasters that might befall us? If you have answers for me I would love to listen on this one... Something is coming and I want to be as prepared as I can be...

Have a great day today, if church, the Mosque, the Synagogue, or Temple is your thing, please say a quiet pray for me, I'll take all I can get these days.

Where have those leaders gone? Where are the men of conviction? Where are the wives of these great men and where are those families that were born from the union of such great folks??

Where is the next MLK Jr.? Did King's words truly only rate as a good speech and some interesting lessons in history classes? Is he only to be an interesting topic in January and then again in February when we watch the films and say, "Was it really that bad then?" "How could they just stand there and let that happen to themselves!" "Why didn't they fight back?" "Did non-violence really work?" Did Dr. King die for nothing?

Is this holiday truly that or is it a token of appreciation so we will stop complaining about things? Why did the episode of the Boondocks spark controversy when it was really about how many of us forgot what the man was really about? Did we forget he was a man of God, who died doing what he believed God wanted him to do? Where is the next MLK Jr.? What happened to real marches about real issues? Where did the SNCC, SCLC, and NAACP go? DO people even remember what "JIM CROW" was?

Dr. King paved the way but when did we stop laying the bricks to the house he built with blood, sweat, tears and his life? When was the last successful boycott after King went home? Something is wrong here, times are supposed to be better. What did he do wrong? Where are the men this great OAK TREE of a man was supposed to Father? King gave his life for what he believed, who picked up his FLAME and added their own lighter fluid? How could we have gone backwards, from Emmit Till to Sean Bell, something is wrong, things were supposed to be better? King saw and understood what the future was supposed to be by looking deep into his present and things still didn't change.
See for yourself-------->

"In a sense we've come to our nation's capital to cash a check. When the architects of our republic wrote the magnificent words of the Constitution and the Declaration of Independence, they were signing a promissory note to which every American was to fall heir.

This note was a promise that all men, yes, black men as well as white men, would be guaranteed the "unalienable Rights" of "Life, Liberty and the pursuit of Happiness." It is obvious today that America has defaulted on this promissory note, insofar as her citizens of color are concerned. Instead of honoring this sacred obligation, America has given the Negro people a bad check, a check that has come back marked "insufficient funds." But we refuse to believe that the bank of justice is bankrupt. We refuse to believe that there are insufficient funds in the great vaults of opportunity of this nation. And so, we've come to cash this check, a check that will give us upon demand the riches of freedom and the security of justice."

—Martin Luther King, Jr.'s *I Have A Dream Speech,*
Washington DC, 1963

Yet nothing has changed and that check was never rewritten. Where did we go wrong? Where is the next MLK Jr.? We are farther divided now than we ever were, economically, educationally, socially and of course spiritually. We are not even close to helping each other over the hump. Hell we have moved back to the back of the bus without being told to do so. How did this happen? Wasn't his death supposed to spark a national uprising that spirited us in the very future he was fighting for, took all those beatings for, and spent time in jail for? I thought when you're a Martyr for your cause people stand up and take notice of your life being taken and become motivated? Where did he fail here?

Did we forget that period between 1963 and 1972 when we watched and allowed America to wild out and kill X, EVERS, The Kennedy Brothers, as well as King? Toss in the infiltration and destruction of all the BLACK Panthers for fun and this is how our movement died? Where did we fail?

Well they gave him a holiday and we get the day off, but through all the TV shows, plays, skits and songs where will the next KING emerge from? The next who, the next KING? One benefit to all this is his queen has left to take her place next to the man she loved so if for nothing else I am happy that the KINGS are reunited. On this day I am going to sit for a few and ponder the very questions I have put to all that have read this. I really don't have the answers.

As an educator I have tricked myself into believing that I will have some small role in the making of the next one (KING), and with the Lord's mercy he'll allow me to see one (KING) grow in the next MLK Jr. I can only dream and pray it doesn't end like the Man who's holiday most won't celebrate in a fashion fitting to the man that died for it become on.

109

Dr. King, I have never met you, nor seen you but your presence is felt when I read your words or watch your videos. The Lord truly touched you and I hope that I can do a tenth of all that you've done to make this a better world to live in. God bless you Dr. King, your wife and your family. I am one of those children who listened to you as I grew into a man and prays someday my children and many other children; *"will one day live in a nation where they will not be judged by the color of their skin but by the content of their character."*

—Martin Luther King, Jr.'s *I Have A Dream Speech,* Washington DC, 1963

However, I have to be honest sir it's not looking to good! GOD BLESS YOU, REVEREND DOCTOR MARTIN LUTHER KING JUNIOR! (1929-1968)

We have become a society of heavy internet usage. Some so much that whole lives are lived out on the internet. Where does all this start? If you never thought about maybe you'll consider why a person chooses their online persona?

SCREEN NAME

Is this what we've become, a group of people who hide behind aliases? What does our choice of screen name say about the person we think we are? Is it really us? Why do so many pick names that have nothing to do with their true personality? Is it the idea of hiding that you really are from the world? We've become so connected to our screen name that we have others calling us by the damn thing in public. Why is this? What does this say about us as a society when our alter egos get more attention than the actual person? In a way its exciting I have been there and watch how people have responded to the name I chose. The smiles that follow kind words simply because they are meeting the *"MADE UP ME,"* but I think it's really me or is it. I truly believe that if I told people my real name they are going to be the same way towards me. However, there are those not like that and this whole process is a sad state of affairs. These are the folks that live and die to be their screen name. They work on developing a persona that is centered on the name of choice.

Think about it, you have the power to take on any name you want. Then dance around the Internet and become anyone you want. Dream of the power this provides a person, to enter chat rooms and become larger then life. To post on message boards and see your name numerous times it's addicting to the less than soul. The internet grants you false power to feel like you're so important when the actual you sits only a push of a button away.

The debate will go on and on and many won't come clean to what their screen name truly means to them. But in my travels the one thing remains true, it's not what you see in a person but what you truly know about a person that tells the story. So the next time when you're emailing, chatting or posting on your favorite boards stop and think what does this name really mean. Who is the person I am talking too? You can take it a little deeper if your not scared, consider what your own screen names mean to you and what role it plays in your life. If you're too wrapped up in the idea of it, then its time to get out of the house and back into creation. Just my thoughts on something we all deal with these days on the internet.

INTERNET POPULARITY

The funny thing with internet popularity is no one really sees you. They won't see the person that you see. They will see what they want and attach whatever feelings towards that vision. This will be based on their wants, likes, needs and their doubts. With onlookers, admirers, and even haters lurking, who is around for you, the real you?

Do they really want to know you or do they just want to get close to the person they made you out to be? Which person is that? Which person is which?

What is the price for this net popularity? I'll tell you since; I am holding a receipt from this net popularity. You will lose being able to speak on your behalf. People will draw their own conclusions and answers, because they'll feel they know you. Your flirting is compared to something decadent. Your smile tells lies or so you have been told. Trust goes out the window because people stop asking what your name is and only mention your screen name.

Hollywood stars and pro athletes are compensated for what they do, so their popularity has a balance. Not so with Net Popularity.

What does someone who has net popularity achieve? The respect from someone posting a positive remark, another person walking up to you at a meet and greet and saying they like or could care less about your style, or the ridicule from someone who doesn't know you, doesn't like who you are and hates what you wrote, simply because that's them. Online, their responses can be vile because their tucked away safely at work or home and hidden behind their own unique screen name.

There is an upside to net popularity, there is having people wanting to get to know you and to see the look of admiration when you walk into the room at an event. The fact many need to gain your approval when conversing on the net can be exhilarating to say the least. The very idea that some have a hint of jealousy because they lack your cyber flare makes you smile. The notion your words move people from many different places to search you out.

The fence is set and if you are net popular you will have to straddle it. If you accept one side, you inherit the other side, like a set of twins. So are you ready to be a parent of Internet Popularity? If you're not sure then you're not ready. I don't have choice my twins won't let me go!

This is a piece for the masses that live on the internet. Who can't get enough of the drug the net can be. Are you an addict?

GUILT & SHAME

Isn't it funny when we make moves the thought about what you just did doesn't hit home until you are truly faced with the repercussions of your actions? Then you are faced with the GUILT or SHAME or both of what you have done. To me, guilt is knowing that you shouldn't have done what you did. As it sits in, your thoughts flowing back and forth "Why did I do that?" Why didn't I stop myself?" "What if it were me at the other end of this pain?" But alas it is done so you deal.

Shame on the other hand is the seeing the damage you have caused and thinking about what you have truly done. It's the poison of your actions reaching its mark and now you are face to face with the cause, yourself!

The two are connected but not everyone gets to the Shame part of the game. Yes many feel guilty but they never reach that point were the feelings hurt so bad they vow "NEVER AGAIN, TO ANYONE ELSE!" and mean it. Most of us never allow ourselves to allow shame to set in because it's a pain that can be overwhelming. When you have to faced anyone with shame in your eyes, face and heart, you don't soon forget it. It actually serves as a measuring stick to your future actions.

I have recently been faced with the shame of some selfless acts, so when you look into the eyes of a woman, child, friend or the mirror, you are forever changed. I am not talking about dealing with guilt I learned how to handle those land mine years ago, but shame is a totally different bomb. It doesn't just hurt your body, your mind but your soul. You hurt in a way that is not easily dismissed or healed... But take this from me, you will heal but you won't be the same trust me. So before you do whatever you're going to do with whomever you're going to do at wherever you're going to do it, take a second and ask "Is this worth the guilt or shame I would have to deal with if the world knew of it?" Then make your choice and may God be there if you ever have to face yourself with "SHAME" present. If it happens to you, contact me. I'll show you how to handle life without getting that comfortable sleep you used to get.

Good Luck

We reach plateaus in our lives and as they approach we start to look deeper at ourselves. A wave of emotions reaches deep into every person. I am no different from anyone else. This is an entry from my attempt at keeping an online journal. I hold on to this because it reminds to stay focus

THE END IS NEAR AND I AM A LITTLE SCARED

Sitting here working and thinking, I am close to the mountaintop and I am a little scared. When you set out to accomplish something some few years earlier and now you're down to the final ten or eleven weeks, your mind and body grow tight. You see, I am finishing my Masters degree in May and it is something I never saw myself achieving.

I still have a few hurdles to overcome before everything is complete but I must say I have to resist the idea of thinking of what it will feel like to get there. The fear of failure has always been a motivational tool for me. But here, I stand, on the cusp of being the first in my immediate family to reach this point. The real funny thing is it's as if all their dreams are tied into my own. My grandmother and mother have done so much and seen so much, to see them pushing and caring so hard you would think they are in school. But in essence they are. I am their child, their only SON and so as the mothers, they are proud.

My sisters aren't as vocal, but just as caring. Their quick comments asking how are you doing or simply leaving me alone when they hear my grandmother say, "The boy got work to do, leave him be," has helped me get to this point of completion. But one of the real reasons I am here is the help of a very special friend. She has dedicated herself to assisting me in doing the one thing I am truly weak at, although I am trying to make a career out of it some day.

That is my writing and her name is Tiffany Braxton. She doesn't like her name in lights. But it's been her support, along with my family, that has gotten me to this point. She will take my ideas and words and shape them into the way I really want them to sound. Every time a Professor writes, "that was a well written paper," I smile and think "THANKS Tiffany!" Her ability to edit the written word has been an asset worth more than platinum. I have learned over this two and a half year Odyssey that anything great takes multiple people to get it done. You may be the person gaining the notoriety, but there are others that have helped you get there. So this is why I am fearful of messing up in the home stretch. I have been thrown a few curves these last few months and I think the moment I breathed a little easier the Devil went to work. But I am focused and determined. As a teacher, the better I do in my personal life the more I have to offer the children who sit and attempt to learn from me. The things I can share with them and seeing their eyes widen helps strengthen my resolve to make this happen.

Then there are my own children all of them, each of my children having their own unique connection to me on different levels. Their future is tied to my success and failures so I am reminded why I can't complain or be tired. It is truly interesting the things that are connected to everything you do and every move you make. It's as if God has designed the model that way.

A life spent trying to figure out what to do and how to handle the effects of what you choose. But I also would be amiss if I didn't mention my ex-Wife, not the way your thinking. It is really easy to dislike or hate someone that you are no longer with. That is not the case with her, she is motivation for me. Many times I feel as if she doesn't respect the man I have become since parting ways. Many of our discussion are not filled with the bounce that regular people have, but when you're divorced are you ever really happy or excited for the other's accomplishments?

I'd like to believe that you can be. I was excited to hear about her finally moving into her own house because I knew that is what she always wanted. The feelings are never returned. Even after five years apart we don't act the way we should. But I can only do what I do and pray she can see past many things to be happy for me. I think our sons would benefit from seeing that a cordial, delightful, friendly union can be held between two that are no longer connected in the marital way. So I am motivated with the idea that she has to at least let my sons know that their dad is doing things in a positive way. Well, I hope she does, but if she doesn't I'll find a way to constantly remind them what this road requires from them to make it. Well I guess this entry is for me, a note to myself to get pass the fear and get back to work. A note to me to "stay on my grind" because so many are rooting and jeering, like an internal and eternal sporting event. The price of winning is high and the price of losing is even higher. I pray that my strength, my health, and all my supports can hold me down as I get closer to the finish line. I pray the souls of my family member not here find a way to nudge me from their perch from way up high. I also pray that the lord give blessings to all those that have gotten here with me, for they deserve more then I could ever give them. Finally I pray that when I wake each day until that final day, my heart and souls stays strong and focused for it is with God's permissions my actions are laid out not my own that decides the ending. Time to get back to work scared or not!

There are times you can look back at yourself and clearly see there is battle raging. I want to allow you too see how the Lord started to reach out to me yet I couldn't completely hear him. It's like being lost and hearing someone calling your name but you're not sure what direction the voice is coming from. In each of us we have a spirit that is connected to so much good that many times we literately get scared when it speaks to us about which direction to head in. Doubt follows because that is what Satan does best. I think you might see yourself as I question what I am doing with me in this piece.

This is one of the pieces I look over and say to myself, does anyone else have these conversations with themselves? I decided to allow others to see into my thought process risking the jeers and snickers. I am sure someone reading will understand the point I was trying to make. Like many I write, I ask that you give it some thought and see where you are with what is said.

K. L.

Getting Out Of My Own Way

I was told at one point in my life from a friend that I was scared of success. I figure this is why I haven't used all my gifts to better myself but to just maintain. I am really trying to understand that about myself and it's very confusing. Here I have a degree from graduate school and what should be the happiest time of my life I'm here feeling incomplete. I can't shake this feeling that there is more that I was meant to do and I am not doing it. I went to the doctor the other day and my sugar levels have returned to where they were supposed to be. I am no longer considered a Diabetic. Everything else was okay Blood Pressure was up a little. But my weight was not cool. I am not going to give the actual number because seeing and hearing it hurts my eyes and ears. I know I have to get on point with things or all this work will have been for nothing because I won't be here. That is the battle most people of size currently deal with.

I really wonder what God has planned for me. I have tapped into some of the gifts he has given me and have tried to learn the ways of the rest that are hidden. But my balance still seems off. I went to see Star Wars the other weekend and I understood Anakin Skywalker's plight, of having to do good while another side of you rages. It's as old as man's reign on this planet, the fight from duality of our souls. Mine just seems to rage on even when I am sleeping. There are days I struggle with being the gentleman I know I am with wanting to be the lust filled whore that I was. The battle of really trying to get rid of this weight to eating everything and saying Why not! With that same voice whispering life is to be enjoyed even if cut short. I know others are fighting their own private and sometime public battles, I am the person they call for help, guidance and support. Who do I run too on my days of weakness? I have turned to the Lord on many occasions since I have seen his powers. But why can't I commit to him like many others whom seem to be saved from what they were. I wonder openly. My life sometimes reminds me of the scene from "The Color Purple" where Shug Avery has made up with her dad and the whole church is rejoicing but there is one sad soul and poor Ms Cecile, clapping and stomping her feet but nonetheless hurting. I am Ms. Celie these days. With all that I have accomplished, I should be happy but something is missing. I have been my own roadblock to what should be a happier existence. Somehow my next quest since school is done is my search for my spirit! Through listening to my soul, writing and hard work I am going to try to become that success that I know I should have been. In whatever area God directs me. Teaching, writing, or counseling I am going to be more of the man that I know I can be. My Nettie will be there for me at some point and I am going to be ready to receive her and the family of blessing she brings. If only I can get out of my own way.

CHOICES

Making observations like many of us do around the New Year, things aren't really making sense... So many people are using this time to reflect on past, present and future situations. Many are starting to work out, eat better and all that... There are those that are going to start and end relationships because it's that time of the year...

What this is really all about is choices and trying to be able to live with the outcomes of those decisions... Doing nothing is a choice just as well as jumping into something head first... People like to use this time because it's the start of a New Year and it appears to be a big time to do so. I am not knocking that. But in my readings of the Bible lately I understand how this free will thing works.

God gave us free will to make choices that will shape our future beds and then we deal one way or another. So many people are stuck inside the memories of poor choices they made so they suffer from feelings that may be surrounding those choices. You will come across it in so many internet blogs this time of year that it might become sickening, but it's their right vent.

Their personal moves have affected them in many ways positive and negative. I have read a few blogs where so many people are still holding on to pure negative feelings from poor choices, sad but I guess it works for them.

I am no different for I have made moves for myself and Bible study is one. I feel I need to understand more than what I am reading. I feel I am strong enough and smart enough to deal with whatever I uncover about the word of God and myself.

This year is going to be a strong choice year; I am planning to make decisions that are well thought out and positive. It won't protect me from negative happenings, but it will lesson the negative outcomes. This past year I have made many negative moves having to deal with them hasn't been easy. I have made decisions that brought people close to me that should have never been there and made it worse by making even poorer move while dealing with them. There have been some positive and outstanding decisions made this year that open the door to a few things that have started to change my life. People, places and things are all a matter of choice, mine will be better.

Have a great morning, afternoon, evening and I hope that your choices or non-choices are blessed. Remember all your actions effect you and those connected to you... I know this may sound simple and rudimentary, but isn't the simplest of choices that hurt the most when they turn negative.

Either way Good Luck

CHAPTER 6

The Man I Used to Be.

For there to be true transition there has to be a point from which you start. This is where I was before the Lord saved me. This man will never see the light of day. This man was in love with the physically aspects of what he could get from a woman. I am ashamed and sad for this man. He was man that didn't love himself so there was no way to love another. I am elated the Lord saved me and changed that man.

Now here we have a section that I wasn't comfortable with adding to the book. As you prepare to read this section, first let me just say this, and I want to say this loudly, that this is who I used to be. This was the type of man that I was before I started to change. I was a man that chased woman for one purpose, a physical purpose. I couldn't make a move towards a woman without having some type of motive in mind to get between her legs, to get inside her pocketbook, whatever it was going to take to get me. Whatever I wanted I was a misogynist. I hated myself because I was unhappy with myself so of course I hated woman. Now some people would ask you were hating woman. Yes, I was hating woman. And I was hating woman because I didn't know to see them

127

as a person. I saw them as an object; a plaything. And when you see something a plaything you treat it with such disrespect. Just like you see kids on Christmas. They play with certain toys and the other ones like they don't even exist. I started to treat woman that way. These poems and stories are reflections of where I was in my life at that point. There are others that I did not place in this section that were just so pornographic that I didn't feel needed to even see the light of day. And I don't think they ever will again. It's just a sad reflection of when you are caught up in flesh and that's another thing that the Lord frees you from, because he strips you of wanting that, because if your focus is on him, it can't be on that. You still think about it, don't get me wrong, I do, but I'm not that. So since you cannot serve two masters, my focus is trying to be the man that God wants me to be. And resisting those feelings, because they don't go away, but you can place them in position. So as you read this section of my book, I hope that you understand that it took a lot of courage and debate to offer these few glimpses of what I used to be. Because I know some church folks might say how could he add this, how could he add this to his manuscript? How could he put this out here to be sold? I'm not selling this section. That is why this section is in the back of the book. It is entitled that. When. So as you read, and I say this boldly, AS YOU READ UNDERSTAND THAT THIS IS GLIMPSE IN THE PAST, AND THAT IS WHERE THAT MAN RESIDES, IN THE PAST. THE

MAN I AM, THE MAN I AM BECOMING, IS THE MAN THAT IS IN THE PREVIOUS PART OF THIS BOOK. THAT MAN IS THE MAN THAT I AM PROUD TO INTRODUCE TO THE WORLD. THE MAN IN THESE NEXT FEW PIECES IS A MAN THAT I WILL NEVER ALLOW OUT. He has been locked up forever. He is serving a life sentence to never be seen again. Because that man was destructive, hurtful, he issued a lot of pain to himself and to others. So as you read, please consider people that you know like this and if you happen to be a person like this, don't ever think that you can't change, because you can. But it requires commitment and work and support and a strong belief in a God who is going to forgive you for being that way, which then allows you to forgive yourself, which is the hardest thing to do when you are that person, and so please enjoy as you read what I used to be.

MY LOVER

It is those eyes that drive me in so many ways.
It is that smile that moves me on rainy days.
It is the chuckle you have after each subtle toke.
It is the freaky look you get whenever you smoke.
It is the sweat that drips to the edge of your chin
It is the taste of your juices when my tongue slides in
It is the moves of your body, pressed hard and then light
It is the feeling of relief as my juices take flight
It is the moan as you slowly move your hips
It is trying to figure which set of lips to kiss
It is the touch of your hands upon my frame
It is the release as you turn and request the same
It is the time spent chilling when two become one
It is finding out that holding each other can also be fun
It is the way you use passion and mix it with lust
It is the way you cradle my heart with a new found trust
It is the loving that has me shaken with a twist
It is the sexy way you lay back and whisper "BIG
DADDY" give me a kiss
It is the reason I lay here and the reason I write
It is You, your mind and your body that has made my
night.

THE GENTLEMAN & THE FREAK

I am the gentleman that holds your hand as we walk down
the street & the freak that will pull your hair until you
scream with delight.

I am the gentleman that will open the door and says after
you & the freak that will sex you until your ***** swells
tight.

I am the gentleman that pulls out your chair and lets you
sit first & the freak that rides you until you have forgotten
my name.

I am the gentleman that picks up the tab when we go to
lunch & the freak that eats you until your **** screams
stop.

I am the gentleman that goes for long rides with you in the
afternoon & the freak that gives it too you on the hood of
the car.

I am the gentleman that loves the walk in the park &
the freak that **** you on a balcony over looking the city.

I am the gentleman that shares with you his deepest

thoughts & the freak that asks real loud whose ***** is this?

I am the gentleman that calls to say I care and I am thinking about you & the freak that comes to your house and **** you against the wall.

I am the gentleman that enjoys a blockbuster night & the freak that gets hard when grinding on you at the club.

I am the gentleman that looks to the sky and yells "THANK GOD, FOR THIS WOMAN!" & the freak that looks to the ceiling yelling "OH god, YOU'RE GOING TO MAKE ME C***!"

I am the gentleman so many want & the freak so many need.

In the end I am what I am The Gentleman & the Freak

This piece speaks to the struggle that each man has going on. My duality was a big draw with the ladies. Being able to switch it off an on got me much more attention. Sexual rewards come to a man or woman who can capture another's interest and excite the dark side at the same time.

A DANCE

Sitting her trying to get my drink on I see you. You look incredible standing there shaking to the music and your eyes are connected to mine. The feeling is so strong I think to myself, is she looking at me? I smile and point to myself and you look back with a nice sexy shy smile. I had to make sure it was me you were looking at. You are a dime and I can't **** this up. Standing up to get myself together and to give you a better look at what I am working with. Looking you over I see your sexy black top, which shows off you're oh so natural beauty. Your shoulders are exposed and looking lovely. It's as if Phyllis Hyman has come back to join us. The form fitting skirt models your full figured shape. Your multiple designed boots highlights the fact you took time to put this look together. This is a Big Beautiful woman in front of me and I am interested.

As I walk over too you trying not to seem eager or a pimp. I think too myself "Please be able to hold a conversation. Please don't be a chicken head. Please don't be one of those "Big Boned" ghetto girls with a great sense of fashion, 5 kids and no dreams. Please do not have a vocabulary that is based constantly on using words like "YOU KNOW WHAT I AM SAYING? YOU KNOW WHAT I MEAN?"

133

I greet you with a firm and masculine "Hello Ms"! Your response is somewhat quiet, "Good evening sir." Sir? Come on now you make me sound older than I am.

I am actually nervous, but I am searching for more words to say. Trying hard not to make myself look foolish... Why is this happening to me? Why is it I can't speak too you? Hell, I am a ladies man, why am I claming up. I say to you, you look incredible tonight. Thank You. I just put something on that was comfortable. Are you here with anyone? Yes, my friend. He is somewhere in here doing his thing, so he left me. That's my opening. Well, Ms., can I make up for his mistake and keep you company until he gets back? Can you? She says as she smiles and giggles provocatively. Damn, what is she doing to me? Why is this woman I have never met moving me like this? Everything around me is a blur; it's all about her. I am sitting here fighting with myself over something I should be running with. This isn't normal for me. I don't even know this girl, why I am getting so off base. Before I could say anything else with a devilish smile I hear, did you come over to talk or to ask me too dance? By all means, would you like too dance with me? Take my hand and follow me to the dance floor. Keep up if you can. Wow here hand is like cotton. I'm flipping. I must have drunk too much; maybe it's the weed they smoke in here. I am paying attention too way too many things. As soon as we hit the dance floor it's on. Our rhythm is such that my moves seem to fit hers. That smile and look, oh my God! She is sexy and moves well. She turns around and I jump on. Yes, a chance to get nears that ample round ass. Its funny I love nothing but big girls and here one of the sexiest I have ever seen is all into me or is it just this heat? God I hope I don't embarrass myself and get excited. I move in closer. She stays right there. She smells terrific. I can't make out the scent, but its paralyzing. I grab her waist not wanting to mess this groove up. I feel her press her ass against me. We are one! I don't want to let go and then she reaches up to caress my face, as if we are engage in some primal mating ritual. You dance well for a big man. Hey, that is an insult. I dance well period. You aren't too bad you're damn self. I see she is digging this closeness as much as I am. I don't remember how many songs past. I lost count. It was almost like a dare, neither want to leave the other. I am in shock. No words were spoken between us but volumes of knowledge were being exchanged on this dance floor. Then the DJ sensing the nature of the way the crowd was dancing cuts into an old Isley Brothers song. Whoa, do I stop? Do I let her go? Do I risk allowing the other sharks in here a chance to supplant me? Should I let them take advantage of the work I put in out here on this dance floor? Hell no! Then she turns too look as if it's up too me if I stay. My eyes say please would you like to finish, that was said with my hand held out. She steps up to this big frame and holds tight. She was pleased that I hadn't given up on this dance yet. Her head rested right at my chest; her height and size complimented mine. Being a big man a small woman was the last thing I wanted. Now I had her close, the grind is slow and steady. Again no words were spoken. In my mind I am trying to make sense of this angel that is in my presence. Why have I not seen her before? Why am I so lucky? Like many men it's hard to just enjoy the moment. But I force myself to stay focused on now and her! Later on is not my concern! As the songs come and end we stayed the course through all of them. She looks and says too me, "I'll be right back" Thinking she was heading to the bathroom I chilled. After a few minutes I get restless. I walk to each end of the club, strolled outside and even peaked in the bathroom to see if I saw her boots in a stall. She was gone! Sitting back at the same stool at the bar, I think too myself. I didn't even ask her what her name was. Damn! Can this really be true? I think I just met "The One" and fell for her just from A DANCE! Damn, I was going to stay home tonight!

A QUICK THOUGHT

I haven't tasted you in months. I am here and you are there. Yes, I said I can deal, but damn my body is not agreeing with the plan right now. I get excited for no reason, just from the thoughts of our last session slips into my mind. How is a brother supposed to work, if the taste of your loins fills his mind? I turned on the TV and Sex and The City was on, damn do I need you right now? I know you love this show and here I am thinking about you again. What was I thinking that night when I said this could work? All I know is your there and I am here. I take a shower and my chest starts to thump from that day in the summer when we both lost our minds. We tried to hurt each other sexually, with the water flowing all over our bodies. Damn, I can still hear your moans as the water careened over your back. I looked down to see my body sliding in and out you. What was I thinking? Did your special place actually have me believing I was super human? Did it have me thinking I could chill and come there every few months or so to do this again? It must be, because I don't want to share our connection with anyone else. I want to be past full strength for you. Because, the next time we make love you're going to sleep first. You're going to be the one waking up deep into our sexual session not vice versa. Wow, the last time we were together I thought I was dreaming when I opened my eyes and you had worked your way on top of me. Only to hear you say so softly, "GOOD MORNING LOVER, NOW RELEASE FOR ME!" Like a child I complied because your private of areas had me tongue-tied. I can't do this. I can't read another sexually charged email or instant message filled of all the things we did, will do and haven't considered yet. Damn, why does good p**** have to seem so far away? It must be me! I went to a party and bugged out when I thought I saw you. Now that is crazy. My body got hard as hell even with the thought of someone else being you. Now that's what's up! So enjoy the day, night or whenever you read this, but now I am tired and I am going to find my way to bed. Damn, what was I thinking?

This was just a Quick Thought.

THE OTHER SIDE OF F***STRATION

F***stration, here I am
Allow me to unleash your womanly desires
Let me take you and lead you to a place of sensual relief
I am, have been, and can be the muse to your sexually
thoughts of passion Give me your mind and watch your
body relax and give in
Trust that sensual souls can connect when called upon
I am the energy you summoned now enjoy yourself
The key to ending your f***stration is sharing your dreams
with a true visionary
I am that teacher, now take my hand and explore your
wants, needs and fantasies.
There will be no more lonely nights with the TV or your
toys because,
F***stration here I am!

THE FUTURE FOR K. L.

It is my prayer that you enjoy this book. As a new writer this was truly a leap of faith for me to place my words out there for the world to judge. I am a man of God and so I am okay with that but the fear doesn't disappear it's just used as motivation to do other things. Faith is a powerful tool that will assist you when dealing with the unknown.

Look for an article of mine on "Love." It will be featured in the August 2008 release of *New York Times* and *Essence* Best Seller Ms. Mary "Honey B." Morrison's *Who Loving You*. Ms. Morrison was kind enough to add me to her novel and I would encourage everyone to check it out. It speaks on how through God and Love of each other, my wife and I were able to overcome my multiple moments of infidelity. My lovely wife caught me four times cheating and we were able to overcome that and remain in love and eventually get married in a perfect wedding and honeymoon. The full story will be in an upcoming project that I am working on. If you want to see the wedding, come by MySpace to see the video and bring some Kleenex.

A Man in Transition

My future projects are entitled:

From Gigolo to Jesus: My Life as a Sexual Predator

A story based on my past as a misogynist until the Lord stepped in and changed my life. I take you on a journey of what a young man does when there is no fatherly guidance and a mother and grandmother trying their best to raise a man. Their failures become other women's pain. Come walk with me as I give the tale of my own path of self-destruction, heartache, pain, and redemption.

Angel with a Devil's Heart

Kevin Watkins is an outstanding school teacher by day and wannabe playboy at night. After not heeding the warning of his childhood friends, he decides to make another man's wife his own. Watch how his world closes in around him as he learns that a jealous husband and jilted mistresses can spell death for someone. You'll have to read to find out who and how. It's a sure fire thriller.

Liberty Prison

Hiding from his past, a teacher of Law with a PhD from Harvard is doing a life sentence for a mistake. Follow along as he tries to hide his identity while looking over mistreated inmates and a student who has been framed and now in the same prison but doesn't know this is his ex mentor. All while dealing with a warden who is using the new experimental prison as million dollar cash machine by using a governmental experimental drug designed to keep prisoners from be aggressive towards each other and it's supposed to leave the prisoners devoid of sexual feelings. But there is a secret the outside world and even the government doesn't know. Find out what the secret of L19 is along with what happens when the teachers cover is blown and how he fights to keep it from getting out who he really is. All this and more happens in the walls of Liberty Prison. A jail like no other in the world.

My hope with my writing is to use my experiences and my imagination to prevent many of the young men in this world from heading down some of the same paths I chose. Many of which they may never recover from in their lifetime. I am also trying to reach the young women, trying to get them to see the signs of a predator that may lurk in their mists. Of course the single mothers and wives who are placing their trust in their partner who may be going out here and placing them both at risk.

I have been in many situations and God saved me to tell the stories. With all that I have done I shouldn't be here to tell you anything. However the Father made me one man with one voice but if you listen I am telling the stories of many. Enjoy the poems and stories they come from my heart and it was step out on faith to present myself to you.

Keep on the look out for my future work. They will be life changers. I thank you again for purchasing this book.

Please don't hesitate to give me your thoughts when we meet. I am a big man I can take it.

Peace, Love and Respect
K. L

www.KLtheWriter.com
MySpace.com/KLthewriter
Email: Kl_the_Writer@yahoo.com

A tribute to my Lovely Wife

Next to the Lord, she is the most important person in my life.

Tiffany Braxton Belvin
My Wife and Plus Size Model

A BIG DOG'S PASSION
Her poem and her words about our relationship
By Tiffany Braxton Belvin aka Mrs. Big Dog

Have you wiped his tears, eased his fears,
or supported his cares?

Do you know his children's names?
Have you been to their sports games? Have you set them
goals to aim?

Have you prayed him up, made his heart jump,
or ever pulled him out of a slump?

Has his family prayed that you will be his wife, bear him
fruit for life,
or had the passion even met that fife?

Have you held his hand, let him be the man,
or took your position at his side when he took a stand?

Have you ever combed his daughter's hair or called her
mother with something to share?

K. L.

Have you ever cheered his team, shared his dreams,
or quelled his quiet screams?

Have you tucked his sons in bed, gave them a place to rest
their head, and then woke up next morning to see them
fed?

Have you ever held him tight, with all your might to make
sure he could sleep at night?

Have you ever dropped to your knees, begged the Father to
hear your pleas, that his soul would be at ease?

Have you ever made it possible for him to think when he
was on the brink of a self-destructive path of life out of
synch?

Have you ever given him hope that he would be able to
cope when things seem to be out of his scope?

Can you tell me what church he was in when he held my
hand as we prayed with the reverend?

All those things are quite relevant when you know
something about a Big Dog's Passion